Gluttony

For over a decade, The New York Public Library and Oxford University Press have annually invited a prominent figure in the arts and letters to give a series of lectures on a topic of his or her choice. Subsequently these lectures become the basis of a book jointly published by the Library and the Press. For 2002 and 2003 the two institutions asked seven noted writers, scholars, and critics to offer a "meditation on temptation" on one of the seven deadly sins. *Gluttony* by Francine Prose is the second book from this lecture series.

Previous books from The New York Public Library/Oxford University Press Lectures are:

Also by Francine Prose

Gluttony

The Seven Deadly Sins

Francine Prose

The New York Public Library

2003

OXFORD
UNIVERSITY PRESS

Oxford   New York
Auckland   Bangkok   Buenos Aires   Cape Town   Chennai
Dar es Salaam   Delhi   Hong Kong   Istanbul   Karachi   Kolkata
Kuala Lumpur   Madrid   Melbourne   Mexico City   Mumbai   Nairobi
São Paulo   Shanghai   Taipei   Tokyo   Toronto

Copyright © 2003 by Francine Prose

Published by Oxford University Press, Inc.
198 Madison Avenue, New York, New York 10016

www.oup.com

Oxford is a registered trademark of Oxford University Press

Library of Congress Cataloging-in-Publication Data

Prose, Francine, 1947–
Gluttony : the seven deadly sins / Francine Prose
p. cm.
Based on a lecture series in the humanities hosted by the New York Public
Library.
Includes bibliographical references.
ISBN 0–19–515699–4
1. Gluttony. I. Title.

BV4627.G5P76 2003
178—dc21

                                                                    2003042045

9 8 7 6 5 4 3 2

Book design by planettheo.com

Printed in the United States of America
on acid-free paper

Contents

Editor's Note

This volume is part of a lecture and book series on the Seven Deadly Sins cosponsored by The New York Public Library and Oxford University Press. Our purpose was to invite scholars and writers to chart the ways we have approached and understood evil, one deadly sin at a time. Through both historical and contemporary explorations, each writer finds the conceptual and practical challenges that a deadly sin poses to spirituality, ethics, and everyday life.

The notion of the Seven Deadly Sins did not originate in the Bible. Sources identify early lists of transgressions classified in the 4th century by Evagrius of Pontus and then by John of Cassius. In the 6th century, Gregory the Great formulated the traditional seven. The sins were ranked by increasing severity and judged to be the greatest offenses to the soul and the root of all other sins. As certain sins were subsumed into others and similar terms were used interchangeably according to theological review, the list evolved to include the seven as we know them: Pride, Greed, Lust, Envy, Gluttony, Anger, and Sloth. To counter these violations, Christian theologians classified the Seven Heavenly Virtues—the cardinal: Prudence, Temperance, Justice, Fortitude, and the theological: Faith, Hope, and Charity. The sins inspired medieval and Renaissance writers including Chaucer, Dante, and Spenser, who personified the seven in rich and memorable characters. Depictions grew to include associated colors, animals, and punishments in hell for the deadly offenses. Through history, the famous list has emerged in theological and philosophical tracts, psychology, politics, social criticism, popular culture, and art and literature. Whether the deadly seven to you represent the most common human foibles or more serious spiritual shortcomings, they stir the imagination and evoke the inevitable question— what is *your* deadly sin?

Our contemporary fascination with these age-old sins, our struggle against, or celebration of, them, reveals as much about our continued desire to define human nature as it does about our divine aspirations. I hope that this book and its companions invite the reader to indulge in a similar reflection on vice, virtue, the spiritual, and the human.

Elda Rotor

Gluttony

Introduction

Several years ago, I was invited to a midtown Manhattan restaurant for a lunch that was part of an ongoing series of gatherings hosted by two women who were writing a book about women's attitudes toward their bodies, eating, diet, weight loss, and so forth. The lunches were designed to enable the writers to talk to groups of women, to hear what women were saying about what they ate and what they didn't eat and how they felt about it—and to pick up clever dieting tips that readers might find useful.

Perhaps a dozen women attended. Some were plump, some were thin, all were attractive and appealing, none was anywhere near obese. But many of them described their relationship with food as a ferocious, lifelong battle for power and control.

The lines were drawn, the stakes were clear. In one corner was the women's resolve, their fragile self-regard, their sense of how they wanted to look and feel, how they wanted the world to see them; in the other corner was the refrigerator and a gallon of chocolate ice cream. One woman described how triumphant she felt when she succeeded in getting her carton of takeout dinner from the store all the way to her house without wolfing it down in the car on the drive home. Another passed along the helpful calorie-counting traveler's trick of calling ahead and asking the hotel at which she would be staying to please empty the mini-bar before she even checked in.

Unsurprisingly, the actual ordering of the lunch was fraught with watchfulness, self-consciousness, and more than a little tension. Decisions were made, minds were changed, requests rethought and altered. How much courage it took simply to ask for the crème brûlée. I can't remember precisely what I ate—it seems to me that everyone started with the salad—but what I do recall is suppressing an impulse to order two desserts just to see what would happen.

It's hard to imagine a similar event occurring in any century besides our own. It seems so quintessentially modern, so current and of the moment. What would Thomas Aquinas or Saint Augustine have made of that lunch, or, for that matter, of a world in which women called ahead with directives concerning the mini-bar contents? And yet, had the event taken place a thousand years in the past—let's say, at an early church council or synod—it would more likely have been recognized for what it really was, as something more substantial than a casual chat about body image and diet. Because in fact, it was a sort of metaphysical discussion, a forum on matters of the body and the spirit. For what were these women talking about except sin and virtue, abstinence, self-control, and the daunting challenge of overcoming the fierce temptations of gluttony?

Of all the seven deadly sins, gluttony has had perhaps the most intriguing and paradoxical history. The ways in which the sin has been viewed have evolved in accordance with the changing obsessions of society and culture. From the early Middle Ages until the early Renaissance, centuries during which mass consciousness was formed and dominated by the tenets of Christianity, the principal danger of gluttony was thought to reside in its nature as a form of idolatry, the most literal sort of navel gazing, of worshiping the belly as a God: a cult with rituals and demands that would inevitably divert and distract the faithful from true, authentic religion.

As the Renaissance and later the Industrial Revolution and eighteenth-century rationalism refocused the popular imagination from heaven to earth and adjusted the goals of labor to include the rewards of this world as well as those of the next, gluttony lost some of its stigma and eventually became almost a badge of pride. Substance, weight, and the ability to afford the most lavish pleasures of the table became visible signs of vitality, prosperity, and of the worldly success to which both the captains and the humble foot soldiers of industry were encouraged to aspire. At the same time, growing concerns (fostered by early writers on health and science) with health and longevity and with keeping the body in some sort of harmonious balance led to an increased interest in diet, moderation, and nutrition.

In the past few decades, as changing notions of physical attractiveness and desirability required that women (and to a somewhat lesser extent, men) be trim and thin, the dictates of beauty culture made gluttony appear as yet another sort of threat. Most recently, our fixation on health, our quasi-obscene fascination with illness and death, and our fond, impossible hope that diet and exercise will enable us to live forever have demonized eating in general and overeating in particular. Health consciousness and a culture fixated on death have transformed gluttony from a sin that leads to other sins into an illness that leads to other illnesses.

These days, few people seriously consider the idea that eating too much or enjoying one's food is a crime against God, a profound moral failure for which we will be promptly dispatched to hell. It's doubtful that even the most devoutly religious are likely to confess and seek absolution for looking forward to breakfast, or having taken pleasure in the delights of last night's dinner.

Yet even as gluttony has (at least in the popular imagination) ceased to be a spiritual transgression, food, the regulation of eating, and the related subjects of dieting, obesity, nutrition, etc., have become major cultural preoccupations. A casual survey of the self-help section of the local bookstore will make it clear how large a place gluttony (in its new, deconsecrated form) now occupies in our collective consciousness. For every volume offering advice about the contemporary equivalents of the other sins (sexual addiction, anger management, and so forth) there are dozens of books designed to help the hapless or self-loathing glutton (itself a notably unfashionable term) to repent and reform.

Meanwhile, the punishments suffered by the modern glutton are at once more complex and subtle than eternal damnation. Now that gluttony has become an affront to prevailing standards of beauty and health rather than an offense against God, the wages of sin have changed and now involve a version of hell on earth: the pity, contempt, and distaste of one's fellow mortals. What makes the glutton's penance all the more public and cruel is that gluttony is the only sin whose effects (in the absence of that rare and fortunate metabolism that permits the fruits of sin to remain hidden) are visible, written on the body. Unlike, say, the slothful, who can, if they wish, manage to appear alert and awake, the modern glutton pays for—and displays—transgression by violating the esthetic norms of a society that places an extreme and even potentially dangerous emphasis on fitness and thinness. In some cases, the punishment for the sin can be nearly as extreme as any suffered by those condemned to eternal damnation. Not long ago, a popular singer arranged to have her stomach stapled—a radical cure for gluttony—in an operation that was broadcast over the internet and could be watched as a kind of punitive mass entertainment.

To trace the evolution of gluttony is to consider where we have come from, where we have arrived, and where we may be heading. For if, as they say, we are what we eat, then how we feel about eating—and eating too much—reveals our deepest beliefs about who we are, what we will become, and about the connections and conflicts between the needs of the body and the hungers of the spirit.

CHAPTER ONE

Is Gluttony a Sin?

Too soon, too delicately, too expensively, too greedily, too much. Those are the five ways in which, according to Gregory the Great—the pioneer enumerator of the seven deadly sins—gluttony reveals itself or, alternately, hides, baiting its trap with the extra portion, the costly delicacy, the tempting between-meals snack.

> Sometimes it forestalls the hour of need; sometimes it seeks costly meats; sometimes it requires that food be daintily cooked; sometimes it exceeds the measure of refreshment by taking too much; sometimes we sin by the very heat of an immoderate appetite.[1]

In fact, Gregory's formulation describes the ways in which most of us eat, or think about eating, or plan to eat—on a more or less daily basis. Of the five warning signs that the sixth-century pope identified as the hallmarks of the sinner, there are really only two—"too greedily" and "too much"—that we continue to associate with gluttony. Does the desire for costly meats or dainty cooking really sound like a crime against God, an evil that should rightly consign us to spend eternity in the third circle of hell? If gluttony is indeed a sin, who among us is not guilty?

Like lust, its sister transgression, the sin of gluttony reflects a constellation of complex attitudes toward the confluence of necessity and pleasure. Unlike the other deadly sins, lust and gluttony are allied with behaviors required for the survival of the individual and the species. One has to eat in order to live; presumably, the race would die out if lust were never permitted to work its magic. And religion has no choice but to acknowledge and accept these self-evident realities.

Because hunger and sexual desire are essential human instincts, even the church fathers—those tireless warriors against the stirrings of biological impulse—were obliged to recognize that lust and gluttony could not be addressed and combated in quite the same ways in which the faithful were advised to struggle against the demons of pride, envy, greed. Sagely, the fourth-century monastic theologian John Cassian referred to these natural proclivities, gluttony and lust, as illnesses that require complex cures.

The traditional solution to the problems of gluttony and lust has been to suggest that the element of sin enters in only when we allow ourselves to relax and *enjoy* satisfying the needs of the body. We are allowed to eat and have sex as long as we don't *like* it. Just as the challenge facing the true believer is to be fruitful and multiply without experiencing lust, so it should be possible to eat without savoring our food. So the notion of gluttony considers the limit of what we need to survive and attempts to disassociate the minimum daily caloric requirement from the contaminating influences of craving, obsession, or pleasure. For both lust and gluttony are less a matter of act than of motive, less of content than of desire, less of impulse than of compulsion.

The fourth-century Desert Father, Evagrius of Pontus—a man whose ascetic regimen in the wilderness was at once a protest against the sin of gluttony and an occasion to spend a considerable amount of time contemplating its nature—has given us perhaps the most comprehensive definition of the sin, not nearly as logical and systematic as Gregory the Great's, but much more lyrical and thrilling:

> Gluttony is the mother of lust, the nourishment of evil thoughts,
> laziness in fasting, obstacle to asceticism, terror to moral purpose,
> the imagining of food, sketcher of seasonings, unrestrained colt,

unbridled frenzy, receptacle of disease, envy of health, obstruction of the (bodily) passages, groaning of the bowels, the extreme of outrages, confederate of lust, pollution of the intellect, weakness of the body, difficult sleep, gloomy death."[2]

Over the centuries, the seriousness, the centrality, the very nature of the sin changed as Judeo-Christian culture underwent a sharpening and an intensification of its innate and essential suspicions about the pleasures of the body. Only in its most recent incarnation (the contemporary horror of overweight, fat, and flesh itself) has the sin of gluttony been neatly separated from most associations with any idea of delight.

Only during the last few decades has the legacy of Puritanism (operating in close partnership with the interests of capitalism) deftly lifted desire and gratification out of the equation, and replaced the notion that humans might *like* eating with the suggestion that we eat principally out of compulsion, illness, self-destructiveness, the desire for self-obliteration, to avoid intimacy and social contact, and so forth. As our cultural concerns have shifted from a focus on religion, God, and the afterlife to an obsession with health and (by extension) the fantasy of endless youth and eternal life, the glutton need no longer fear a punitive afterlife but, rather, death itself—a premature death caused by immoderation, excess, and slovenly self-indulgence.

The superheroes of gluttony—from Gargantua to Diamond Jim Brady—have been relegated to the distant, benighted, unenlightened past. Their heirs—today's big eaters—are commonly regarded as freaks or sociopaths, or, even more commonly, as ordinary losers, misfits, unfortunate human specimens. On occasion, the hugely obese (in whom we may see frightening images of what might happen to us if we stopped heeding the promptings of social control and our own shaky superegos) are featured on the evening news, in prime-time versions of the midway side show. Often, these "news" stories concern some hapless man or woman who has grown so wide that he or she can no longer leave the house without a team of carpenters being called in to widen the doorways.

The public loves and despises the spectacle of those male and female movie stars and divas who gain and lose prodigious amounts of weight. When Liza Minnelli was married in the spring of 2002, it was widely reported that the bride had lost 90 pounds in preparation for the nuptials. These days, if you're overweight the last thing it seems to mean is that you have a passion for the tastes and flavors of food.

Yet, for all its abhorrence of tiny weight gains and minuscule accretions of body fat, the culture is fixated on identifying the trendiest restaurant and the newest exotic ingredient. What results is often the phenomenon of rich, thin, young people eating tiny and absurdly expensive portions, or worse, of young women whose understandable difficulty in interpreting the conflicting messages dispatched by the larger society contributes to the development of a host of common eating disorders. What's generally agreed upon now (at least in the popular imagination) is that the compulsive eaters, the modern-day gluttons, have some outstanding "issues" involving low self-esteem or past abuse, some bottomless void they are trying to fill by binging on massive infusions of unhealthy, fattening food.

However flawed and partial, the idea that overeating is symptomatic of a psychological disorder somehow seems (at least to the secular mind) more logical and comprehensible than the notion that gluttony should constitute a crime against the divine order. Who in the world first decided that gluttony was a *sin?* The sensible question that recurs in discussions of this particular deadly sin is: Whom exactly does it harm except the glutton himself? Admittedly, the act and the physical consequences of gluttony can be intensely unattractive, but the sin is not nearly so esthetically unappealing as, say, the more repugnant and shaming spectacles of sloth, avarice, and envy. Nor is gluttony so plainly dangerous as pride and anger, which can so easily lead to discord, violence, social chaos.

One can imagine a certain ease, a certain sureness surrounding the choices that the church fathers were obliged to make as they decided what to include on the list of the seven deadly sins. Pride and anger must have been obvious candidates. Envy and lust can wreak havoc, leaving corpses in their wake. But who, exactly, will suffer if, in that one tiny moment of self-forgetting, we help ourselves to that second or even third helping of pecan pie?

How did overeating come not merely a vice but one of the cardinal vices, with the associated reputation for corruption and contagion, a sin that leads to other sins, a gateway sin to further evil? Saint Augustine suggests—without much explanation—that gluttony leads to flattery. Possibly he is thinking of the fawning lies people tell in order to secure an invitation to a famously lavish and generous table.

For the most part, the reasoning of the early theologians concerning the contaminating nature of gluttony tends to fall into two categories, with two sets of arguments that are by no means mutually exclusive.

The first principal objection to gluttony is that worship of the senses in general and of the sense of taste in particular turns our attention from holy things and becomes a substitute for the worship of God. The phrase that recurs in sermons and warnings against gluttony is the metaphor of the belly as God, as the object of reverence and devotion. Saint Paul takes up this theme in his Epistle to the Romans (Rom. 16:17): "Now I beseech you, brethren, mark them which cause divisions and offenses contrary to the doctrine which ye have learned; and avoid them. For they that are such serve not our Lord Jesus Christ, but their own belly and by good words and fair speeches deceive the hearts of the simple." He returns to the subject in his Epistle to the Philippians (Phil. 3:18-19): "For many walk, of whom I have told you often, and now tell you even weeping, that they are the enemies of the cross of Christ. Whose end is destruction, whose God is their belly, and whose glory is in their shame, and who mind earthly things."

The second theory is that gluttony makes us let down our guard, weakens our moral defenses, and thus paves the way for lechery and debauchery, an argument that seemed especially cogent during those centuries when the term "gluttony" signified not only excessive eating (as it is mostly understood today) but also overindulgence in drink. For Saint Basil the link between gluttony and lust was fairly direct, as "through the sense of touch in tasting—which is always seducing toward gluttony by swallowing, the body, fattened up and titillated by the soft humors bubbling uncontrollably inside, is carried in a frenzy towards the touch of sexual intercourse."[3]

In arguing for the inclusion of gluttony among the deadly sins, the sins that lead to other sins, Aquinas lists the "six daughters" that overeating is likely to spawn: "excessive and unseemly joy, loutishness, uncleanness, talkativeness, and an uncomprehending dullness of mind."[4] Overindulgence, it was generally agreed, offered an open invitation to lust, anger, and sloth. In other words, the six daughters crop up in our behavior when we're drunk or stuffed with food, when we have eaten ourselves into a state of consciousness—or unconsciousness—in which we've stopped thinking rationally and have begun to act in ways that look better from the inside than the outside.

According to a popular medieval legend, the hermit John of Beverley was tested by God, who sent an angel to force John to choose among three sins: drunkenness, rape, or murder. Sensibly, as anyone might, the hermit chose drunkenness. Or not so sensibly, as it would soon turn out, because, in his drunken insensate stupor, he raped and murdered his own sister.

In Chaucer, the tale told by the vain, corrupt, proudly unrepentant, and sexually ambiguous Pardoner is, in theory, an illustration of the principle that greed (a sin with which the mercenary Pardoner is presumably acquainted on a firsthand basis) is the root of all evil. But as it happens, greed is only a sort of byproduct of the real sin at the dark heart of this tale, which, of course, is gluttony.

Part narrative, part sermon, part parody of a sermon, the Pardoner's charged, overheated rant is a haunting, spooky evocation of the daughters of gluttony, the violent and chaotic horrors to which eating and drinking can lead. In that way, it resembles the story of John of Beverley: bloody-minded evidence that the deceptively innocuous sin of gluttony is the mother of far worse evil. It functions as a sort of quick march, a breathless tour through past and popular arguments against overeating and drinking, railings from earlier centuries that were doubtless still heard, in Chaucer's era, from actual individuals more or less exactly like the Pardoner.

The Pardoner begins by describing a group of young debauchees in Flanders, heavy eaters and serious drinkers, profaners, frequenters of taverns, clients of the prostitutes and dancers who work to

> kindle and blow upon the fire of lechery
> That is attached to Gluttony.
> For the holy Scripture I take as my witness
> that lust is in wine and drunkenness.[5]

The Pardoner breaks off his narrative to call upon biblical authority. He cites the story of Noah, who drank so much that he failed to notice that he was sleeping with his own daughters, and the crime of Herod who, when drunk, allowed himself to be persuaded that John the Baptist should be beheaded. For good measure and to marshal additional evidence in support of his case, he cites the classics, tossing in Seneca's remark on how hard it is to distinguish a drunk man from a mad one.

By now the Pardoner has nearly forgotten the three revelers of Flanders, so far gone is he into the sort of preaching that would have convinced his food-and-drinking loving listeners that they desperately needed the absolution that could be purchased along with the Pardoner's holy relics. His sermon is like an aria, during which the pitch keeps rising to a series of crescendos, apostrophes, and pure imprecation:

> Oh gluttony, full of cursedness
> Cause of our first ruin
> O root of our damnation.[6]

Soon enough, the Pardoner's rhetorical detour takes him all the way back to Adam and Eve, who lived blissfully in Paradise while they continued to fast but who were cast out for their gluttony, for eating the fruit of the forbidden tree. "O, if a man knew how many miseries followed from excess and gluttony, He would be more moderate in his diet when he sits at the table. Alas, the brief pleasure of swallowing, the tender mouth makes men— north and south, east and west—work to satisfy their gluttonous tastes for meat and drink."[7] The Pardoner quotes Saint Paul on the subject, then soars into a denunciation of the grossness of the body: "O womb, O belly, O stinking bag, filled with dung and corruption. At either end of thee, foul is the sound . . . "[8] And so the

Pardoner goes on and on, describing the typical drunkard (ugly, sour-breathed, hideous to embrace) and refusing to let up until he's reached the story of the death of Attila, who "died in his sleep with shame and dishonor, bleeding drunkenly from the nose."[9] After a brief meditation on the evils of gambling and swearing, the Pardoner returns to pick up the thread of his narrative.

The three drunkards of Flanders hear the tolling of the death knell, and, apparently too inebriated to identify the sound, they ask what it is. On being told that Death, aided by his helper, the Plague, has been making considerable headway in the neighborhood, they take a vow to find and kill Death. As they stumble along on their way they meet a mysterious old man who directs them to a tree under which, he says, they will find Death. But what they find instead are eight bushels of gold florins. They (drunkenly) decide to stay under the tree until nightfall, when they can remove the gold safely without being seen, and they send the youngest of the three revelers to town to bring back more food and drink.

While he's gone, the two left behind conspire to murder the third upon his return so there will be more gold for them—an idea that has, unfortunately, already occurred to their young friend, who returns with jugs of poisoned wine. After they kill their friend, the two remaining revelers celebrate by drinking the poisoned wine, which of course proves fatal. And so they have found Death after all, and in the process have worked their way through all the sins—anger, treachery, stupidity, pride, greed, and finally murder—that can be spawned by the deadly sin of gluttony, of drunkenness and overindulgence.

Chaucer's portrayal of the gluttons and revelers is not unlike the representation of gluttony that appears in another fourteenth-century work, William Langland's *The Vision of Piers Plowman*:

> Gluttony he gave also and great oaths together,
> All day to drink at divers taverns,
> There to jangle and jape and judge their fellow Christians.
> And on fast days to feed before the full time
> And then sit and sup till sleep them assail,
> And to breed like town swine and repose at their ease
> Till sloth and sleep make slek their sides;
> And Despair to awaken them so with no wiall to amend;
> They believe themselves loast. This is their last end.[10]

In his *Imitation of Christ*, Thomas à Kempis summed up the matter even more succinctly: "When the belly is full to bursting with food and drink, debauchery knocks at the door."[11] So naturally we cannot be mindful of God or of our final end or even of our human nature or moral responsibilities when, carried away by gluttony, we are behaving like the animal that came to symbolize the sin—that is to say, the pig.

How did the odd, long, and enduring career of gluttony make it seem so much more serious than one of those secret failings that the sinner might worry about in the quiet of the night, at that moment when one wakes consumed with regret over that extra lamb chop, the second bowl of rice pudding? How did gluttony graduate beyond the personal list of character flaws that the penitent might whisper about in the privacy of the confessional—and how did it become, as it is today, the most excruciatingly public of the sins, the nearly unforgivable crime against the self and society that, like Hester Prynne's scarlet A, is worn constantly, a badge of shame that not only brands the wrongdoer but, like the evil space creature from *Alien*, comes to inhabit the sinner's own body? How did gluttony—and the related issues of thinness, body image, weight, eating disorders, and so forth—become such a widespread and all-consuming cultural obsession that if we define sin, as a number of the church fathers did, as the cause and subject of inordinate and extreme interest and desire, then by that logic we have become a nation of gluttons, a society of sinners?

Like Chaucer's Pardoner, those who have wished to establish a lineage for gluttony, to trace its roots back to the beginnings of Judeo-Christian tradition have claimed that the urge to commit gluttony was among the promptings that tempted Adam and Eve to taste the forbidden fruit. In her thoughtful study of medieval fasting, *The Burden of the Flesh*, Teresa M. Shaw quotes the early church philosophers who—like the Pardoner—argued that if Adam had only practiced abstinence or moderation, we would all still be gamboling naked, enjoying the fruits of the garden, and naming the animals in Eden. Furthermore, the church fathers preached, those Christians who took up fasting might miraculously be granted return to the lost purity of Paradise.

This interpretation of Adam's fall is also often cited in the gluttony-leads-to-lechery arguments against excessive eating and drinking. First Adam and Eve ate the apple, then they discovered sex. Gluttony, then lust. It might be argued more logically that one bite of an apple hardly constitutes gluttonous eating or drinking, or the sort of eating orgy (such as the one portrayed in Tony Richardson's film version of *Tom Jones*) that can shift so seamlessly from the table to the bed. To not understand that Adam and Eve's sin was disobedience seems somehow to miss the point of that part of Genesis. In any case, the serious gluttons in Eden would more likely have consumed the entire *crop* of the tree of knowledge.

Preachers, theologians, and more recently the designers of Christian web sites scour the Bible for warnings against gluttonous overindulgence but fail to come up with much besides the negative reference to the drunkenness of Noah, as well as general praise for the virtues of moderation and admonitions to treat the body as the temple of the Holy Ghost. Proverbs 23:20-21 advises us: "Be not among winebibbers; among riotous eaters of flesh. For the drunkard and the glutton shall come to poverty and drowsiness shall clothe a man with rags." Yet somehow the image of winebibbers and riotous eaters of flesh fails to correspond to the sin we face, left alone with the mashed potatoes. When Deuteronomy advises that the wayward son be denounced by his parents as a drunkard and a glutton, and subsequently stoned to death by the general populace, the accusation of gluttony seems merely a fillip, an add-on to the son's real sin, which is seditiousness and disobedience—rebellion against the authority of the parents and by extension, against God.

And when Proverbs enumerates the things that God hates— a proud look, a lying tongue, hands that shed innocent blood, a heart that deviseth wicked imaginations, feet that run to mischief, a false witness, he that soweth discord among brethren—it will be noted that the glutton and the overfull stomach are nowhere among them. Ecclesiastes 10:17 warns against overindulgence: "Blessed art thou, O land, when thy king is the son of nobles, and thy princes eat in due season, for strength, and not for drunkenness!" But more common is the counsel that runs through the book like a sort of refrain (Eccles. 2:24): "There is nothing better for a man, than that he should eat and drink, and that he should make his soul enjoy good in his labor. This also I saw, that it was from the hand of God."

Indeed, most of the feasting in the Old and New Testaments is, as it should be, celebratory, unclouded by guilt, regret, or remorse. Famine was properly dreaded, banquets were held to make peace and to mark victories, to welcome guests and send guests on their way. Feasts were ordered to mark the conclusion of the seven days during which unleavened bread was to be eaten in commemoration of the exodus from Egypt; set feasts and burnt offerings were prescribed in the Book of Numbers. The story of Esther concludes with a day of feasting to celebrate the Jews' deliverance from the evil conspiracies of Haman. Isaiah describes the final feast of wines and of fat things full of marrow that will accompany our ultimate redemption.

When Jesus performs the miracle of the loaves and fishes, no one seems to have been looking on with disapproval, ready to condemn those in the crowd who might have helped themselves to extra bread and fish. In a line that would play a critical role in the church fathers' subsequent discussions of gluttony, Jesus says quite plainly that we cannot be defiled by what we eat. Quite possibly this was meant to have a political significance, to serve as a way of separating Christianity from Judaism, with its elaborate dietary laws. In any case, this passage from the Scriptures became a sort of touchstone for those who would argue that what (and by extension, how much) the good Christian put in his stomach mattered less than what he had in his soul and in his heart.

In the Greco-Roman tradition, feasting, along with drinking, was the social cement that enforced the values of the citizen and kept the state together. Good feasts and the bad feasts are recurring motifs at the center of the *Odyssey*, where it is made very clear that the worth of the host depends upon the generosity of his table. At the same time, the *Odyssey* is filled with barely encrypted warnings about the perils of excess; only after having made the Cyclops drunk and slow-witted are Odysseus and his men enabled to blind him and escape from his cave—to evade his plans to eat *them*.

Like so many of the philosophers and theologians who would come after him, Aristotle counseled moderation in eating and drinking:

> Drink or food that is above or below a certain amount destroys the health, while that which is proportionate both produces and increases and preserves it. So too is it, then, in the case of temperance and courage and the other virtues. For the man who flies from and fears everything and does not stand his ground against anything becomes a coward, and the man who fears nothing at all but goes to meet every danger becomes rash; and similarly the man who indulges in every pleasure and abstains from none becomes self-indulgent, while the man who shuns every pleasure, as boors do, becomes in a way insensible;

temperance and courage, then, are destroyed by excess and defect, and preserved by the mean.[12]

And Plutarch compares the body to a ship that must not be overloaded with food and drink, or it will founder and go under.

Such sensible warnings, apparently, failed to have much effect on celebrations staged during the heyday of the Roman Empire, when thoughtful hosts installed their infamous vomitoriums to make sure that nothing would limit the guests' capacity for enjoyment. As we shall see, such works as Petronius's *Satyricon* delight in detailing the porcine excesses to which its partygoers went and invite the reader to laugh at the ludicrously lavish meal the ex-slave Trimalchio serves his acquaintances, the huge platter arranged with dishes designed to correspond to the signs of the zodiac—the testicles and kidneys for Gemini, the lobster for Capricorn. Trimalchio sends a pack of hunting dogs tearing into the dining room as a way of introducing the pièce de résistance, the roast wild boar wearing a hat. Even if we conclude (as we're meant to) that this ridiculous feast is indicative of the same coarseness and vulgarity that makes the ex-slave take an ex-whore as his consort and hire a pretty boy to distribute bunches of grapes while singing nasal hymns to the gods of food and wine, none of us—certainly not Petronius—are ready to suggest that Trimalchio should be tortured, for time and all eternity, for the sin of encouraging his guests to eat too well and too much.

Among the early Christians' responses to the world around them was a certain righteous disgust at the decadence of the Romans' excesses. So Tertullian expressed his horror at the mass belching that soured the air at the lavish feasts, the debts incurred by the degenerate families each time they assembled for dinner. Again, ideas about diet, about abstinence and indulgence were used to draw religious-political boundaries. Much of Tertullian's impassioned and lengthy defense of fasting is based on a reading of the Bible that essentially blames many of the most serious transgressions in the Old Testament—starting with Adam's fall—on the inability of the Hebrews to control their appetites and to moderate their diets. And he (indeed, somewhat graphically) cites the basic facts of human anatomy to explicate the close relationship between gluttony and lust:

> Lust without voracity would certainly be considered a monstrous phenomenon; since these two are so united and concrete that, had there been any possibility of disjoining them, the pudenda would not have been affixed to the belly itself rather than elsewhere. Look at the body: the region of these members is one and the same. In short, the order of the vices is proportionate to the order of the members. First, the belly; and then immediately the species of all other species of lasciviousness are laid subordinately to daintiness: through love of eating, love of impurity finds passage.[13]

The essential disgust for the body that percolates up through the passage above was repeated, with variations, through the works of many of the early theologians who addressed the issue of gluttony; they would reappear, as we have already seen, in such works as "The Pardoner's Tale." John Chrysostom rather graphically identified the symptoms and signs of gluttony: "Discharge, phlegm, mucus running from the nose, hiccups, vomiting, and violent belching. . . . The increase in luxury is nothing but the increase in excrement."[14]

Too soon, too delicately, too expensively, too greedily, too much. It was gluttony's misfortune that the codifying of the virtues and vices coincided with the first flowering of the Christian monastic movement and with the simultaneous growth of the idea that the body was to be ignored, denied, despised, and even, if necessary, mortified into submission. The pleasure haters and monastery dwellers (and those whose worldview placed them squarely in both categories) naturally conspired to put gluttony on the same list as lust—two impulses that, if allowed to erupt uncontrolled, would certainly hinder the smooth operation of a very particular kind of institution. Even as the church fathers were devoting pages and hours of debate to the fine points of lust, to the delicate distinctions between sinful and pardonable ways of having sex, so the increasing hatred for human physicality naturally began to focus on eating—the other principal source of sensual pleasure.

Interestingly, the glutton never managed to inspire the same ferocity of revulsion—or for that matter, the same degree of interest—as the fornicator and the adulterer. But the saints and clerics understood that similar forces were at work, and they labored to make sure that comfort and delight should not get in the way of the austere devotions, the pure concentration that true Christians were meant to reserve for God.

According to an early biography of Francis of Assisi, the saint used ashes as a spice with which he sprinkled his food in order to destroy any hint of taste. For Augustine, the battle to subdue the urge to take delight in eating presented nowhere near the challenge of the corresponding struggle to remain chaste, and yet it posed the same problem: how to avoid the lures of enjoyment. In the tenth chapter of the *Confessions,* he begins his consideration of the sin by citing the obvious fact: that it is necessary to eat. He notes that by eating and drinking we repair our bodily decay, in a kind of daily race with Death, until inevitably Death wins, and the corruptible body is at last clothed in the raiments of the spirit that remains pure for all eternity.

Augustine speaks of food as a medicine we are required to take; but the tricky part is navigating the distance between hunger to repletion with falling, along the way, into the snare of concupiscence. The bare minimum necessary for health is—as Augustine remarks and as every dieter knows—often too little for pleasure. The saint takes pride in the fact that he is not tempted to drink too much, so that refraining from drunkenness represents a far less costly victory than the triumph over the siren song of food. He cites exemplary cases as a way of distinguishing between those instances in which gluttony did, and did not, lead to other sins. Citing Noah, who after the flood was permitted to eat any flesh that could possibly be eaten, and John the Baptist surviving on locusts in the wilderness, Augustine points out that these were obviously very different situations than that of Esau, who sold his birthright for a mess of porridge. John the Baptist's unusual dietary preference was nowhere near as reprehensible as the sin of the Hebrews, who, while wandering in the desert, committed the ultimate evil of being so concerned with their bellies that it turned them away from God.

"But full feeding," the saint writes, endearingly, "sometime creepeth upon thy servant."[15] It is, as Augustine well understands, a common enough failing: Who, Lord, he asks, has not been tempted to eat a little more than he needs? He makes the distinction that began with Christ himself and reached its height with Aquinas: that what truly matters is not what one eats but the spirit and the manner in which one eats it. It's a distinction he expounds upon further in *On Christian Doctrine:*

For it is possible that a wise man may use the daintiest food without any sin of epicurism or gluttony, while a fool will crave for the vilest food with a most disgusting eagerness of appetite. And any sane man would prefer eating fish after the manner of our Lord, to eating lentils after the manner of Esau, or barley after the manner of oxen. For there are several beasts that feed on commoner kinds of food, but it does not follow that they are more temperate than we are. For in all matters of this kind it is not the nature of the things we use, but our reason for using them, and our manner of seeking them, that make what we do either praiseworthy or blameable.[16]

"I fear not the uncleanness of meat," Augustine notes in the *Confessions,* "but the uncleanness of desire."[17]

Too soon, too delicately, too expensively, too greedily, too much. Is the sin of gluttony really only an offense against the self and the body—or can it also constitute a wrong against society? In search of an answer perhaps we should turn from Augustine's confession (or *testimony,* as Garry Wills more accurately terms it in his recent biography of the saint) to my own.

How often the modern confession takes the form of the account of one's most embarrassing moment, told and retold until it has lost, or almost lost, its power to embarrass. My own story, as it happens, concerns gluttony. The particular occasion for sin was a social event in which I unconsciously or semiconsciously hurt others by my rather moderate (if I may say so) descent into gluttony.

The event was a poetry reading hosted by a famous artist, and to which my husband and I had been invited by a friend, who also happened to be the famous artist's former girlfriend. We arrived to find fifty people or so gathered in the top level of the artist's duplex loft, sitting on the wooden floor and waiting expectantly for the poets to begin their recitations.

Most of the poets seemed to be current or former girlfriends of the famous artist. And their poems were, more often than not, heartfelt tributes to his genius, in the studio and in bed. It was an excruciating performance that seemed to last forever, until finally someone said, "Okay everyone, let's go downstairs and have some beer and oysters." We trooped down to the artist's living quarters, where there was a huge tub full of beer and, we assumed, oysters. There was also a table on which there were three plates, each of which contained a dozen opened oysters.

Perhaps our subsequent behavior might make more sense if I explain that just a week before, we had attended a wedding at which there was an oyster bar with a seemingly unlimited supply of bivalves. As in some medieval glutton's paradise, the supply of shellfish appeared magically to replenish itself with every clam or shrimp that we ate. Perhaps our memory of this feast clouded and distorted our perception of the reality of what turned out to be an entirely different situation.

In any case, our friend, my husband, and I decided to do the right—the polite, the socially responsible—thing. We would each help ourselves to a beer, then make our way to the table, at which we would each eat our dozen or so oysters, and then leave to make room for the other guests to likewise have their fill.

Which is essentially what we did. Until we clearly heard someone say, "They've eaten *all* the oysters." We turned to see that the tub we'd assumed to be full of beer and oysters contained, in fact, only beer. Had we imagined the oysters? Or had our clear sights been dimmed by a faint haze of hostility generated by the cruelly protracted poetry reading? I have never been completely sure. Mostly what I remember is how quickly we left the party, and my sense of how we must have looked, as hurried and guilty as Adam and Eve fleeing Eden in a Renaissance painting.

While it may seem that gluttony is a personal crime that involves only the self, the introduction of a situation in which there is a limited food supply—as there is, at every moment, if we consider our planet to be such a situation—makes gluttony seem more serious: a sin against one's fellow human beings and against humanity in general. So it begins to seem more like anger and sloth—volatile, irresponsible, threatening, and at the very least unproductive. Consequently, it's hardly surprising that as Christianity became—as religions tend to—an instrument of social control as well as a spiritual discipline, when men and women began living in convents and monasteries, gluttony assumed pride of place in the hierarchy of deadly sins.

This was especially relevant for those early church fathers who were less interested in the vagaries of the individual soul than in the broader and more concrete requirements of running a social institution, especially that tricky one: a domestic confraternity in which a large group of theoretically celibate men were supposed to co-exist in peace and harmony. It comes as no surprise that the Benedictine Rule is very clear on, and meticulously detailed about, the regulations pertaining to the dinner hour:

> An hour before meal time let the weekly servers receive each a cup of drink and a piece of bread over the prescribed portion, that they may serve their brethren at the time of refection without murmuring and undue strain. On solemn feast days, however, let them abstain till after Mass.
>
> Making allowance for the infirmities of different persons, we believe that for the daily meal, both at the sixth and the ninth

hour, two kinds of cooked food are sufficient at all meals; so that he who perchance cannot eat of one, may make his meal of the other. Let two kinds of cooked food, therefore, be sufficient for all the brethren. And if there be fruit or fresh vegetables, a third may be added. Let a pound of bread be sufficient for the day, whether there be only one meal or both dinner and supper. If they are to eat supper, let a third part of the pound be reserved by the Cellarer and be given at supper. If, however, the work hath been especially hard, it is left to the discretion and power of the Abbot to add something, if he think fit, barring above all things every excess, that a monk be not overtaken by indigestion. For nothing is so contrary to Christians as excess, as our Lord saith: "See that your hearts be not overcharged with surfeiting."[18]

To understand the importance of these strictures, you need only imagine the refectory of the monastery. The monks are waiting at the table. The brothers who work in the kitchen appear with bowls of gruel, loaves of bread, perhaps even the platters of meat; considerable evidence exists that the medieval diet was richer and more carnivorous than we tend to assume. Let us imagine that each monk has taken his share, and that there is just enough food for each one, or in any case the amount that the monastery has decided is appropriate for each one. And let us further imagine that perhaps by some miscalculation one extra portion is left over, and that one monk—perhaps the same one every evening—blithely helps himself to the remaining portion, while the others watch with . . . what? Disgust or contempt, envy or anger. So gluttony *can* be the mother of further sin, and is it any wonder that, under the circumstances, John Cassian placed it at the head of his roster of faults that must be overcome.

Cassian, a fourth-century monastic, founded holy orders for men and women near Marseilles and devised a code of conduct for their daily routine and for the operation of the monastery. His inventory of the eight principal vices would later form the basis for Gregory the Great's list of seven deadly sins. He was also the proponent of an early form of what we have come to call muscular Christianity; many of his metaphors describe the overcoming of sin as something like a formal wrestling match performed by "athletes of Christ."

"And so," he wrote, "the first conflict we must enter upon is that against gluttony" because "we cannot enter the battle of the inner man unless we have been set free from the vice of gluttony." We cannot begin to undertake the "Olympic" contests against our vices, we cannot start to wage war against our spiritual failings until we have overcome our carnal desires. "For it is impossible for a full belly to make trial of the combat of the inner man: nor is he worthy to be tried in harder battles, who can be overcome in a slight skirmish." For Cassian, too, lust is at the end of the natural progression of vices set in motion by gluttony, and he stresses the importance of bridling sensual temptation: "Do not pity the body bitterly complaining of weakness, nor fatten it up with extravagant food. . . . For if it recovers, it will rise up against you and it will wage battle against you without truce. . . . A body deprived of food is an obedient horse, and it will never throw off its rider."[19]

Another early theologian, Saint John Chrysostom, a popular preacher known for his "golden voice" and whose sermons on occasion soared to lofty heights of anti-Semitism and misogyny, was considerably less tolerant than John Cassian in his condemnation of the gluttonous impulse—a temptation he traced back to the doubting, ungrateful, manna-gobbling Jews in the wilderness. In fact, he saw Jewish gluttony as one of the principal obstacles preventing the Hebrews from converting en masse to Christianity.

> There is nothing worse, nothing more shameful, than gluttony; it makes the mind gross and the soul carnal; it blinds, and permits not to see clearly. Observe, for instance, how this is the case with the Jews; for because they were intent upon gluttony, entirely occupied with worldly things, and without any spiritual

thoughts, though Christ leads them on by ten thousand sayings, sharp and at the same time forbearing, even thus they arise not, but continue groveling below.[20]

The way Chrysostom reimagines the conversation between Christ and the Jews on the subject of whether manna came from Moses or from God makes it sound like a quibble between foodies on the true nature of bread. "'They, when they heard this, replied, 'Give us this bread to eat'; for they yet thought that it was something material, they yet expected to gratify their appetites, and so hastily ran to Him. What doth Christ. Leading them on little by little, He saith 'The bread of God is He which cometh down from heaven, and giveth life unto the world.'"[21] Elsewhere, the "golden-voiced" one attempts to scare his audience into abstinence by threatening them with the horror of being found inferior to women—young virgins who seem to have no difficulty in fasting.

By the time Saint Thomas wrote his *Summa Theologica*, gluttony had made its way up to near the top of the list of the seven deadly sins and—in its probable consequences—down to the third circle of hell. So Aquinas was moved to answer, in his rhetorical fashion, the imaginary objections of those who might have been slow to grasp the less-than-apparent connection between food and eternal damnation.

Aquinas begins by quoting the words of Jesus in response to the Pharisees who accused him of heresy because Jesus and his disciples did not wash their hands before eating—an essential aspect of Jewish dietary rules and communal tradition that Christ and his apostles willfully ignored. Presumably, this rejection of established tradition reflected the sensible intuition that—respecting or breaking food taboos and laws regarding cuisine—represented an important way of establishing a collective identity and of defining the other.

It is in this context that Jesus delivers his pronouncement: What goes into our mouths cannot defile us, but what comes out of our mouths—presumably, he means lies, evil thoughts, killings, seductions, false witness, blasphemies, and forth—certainly can. Aquinas interprets this to mean that *nothing* we put in our mouths can defile us, so gluttony—which essentially means putting everything we can grab hold of into our mouth, *too soon, too delicately, too expensively, too greedily, too much*—cannot defile us either. Aquinas points out that Jesus' distinction did indeed refer to the dietary laws; then he explains why gluttony *should* be a danger—it's not the food or the eating—what we actually consume—it's not what we put in our mouths, but the *inordinate desire* for food, a longing so powerful and thoroughly involving that it comes between us and God.

Perhaps Aquinas's notably soft line on gluttony may have had something to do with the fact that the saint was said to have had what today we might call a weight problem. Indeed he seems to have been the twelfth-century version of the nineteenth-century industrialist Diamond Jim Brady, who was said to know that he had eaten enough when his belly had swelled to span the distance that, at the start of the meal, he'd left between his stomach and the edge of the table. According to G. K. Chesterton, "His bulk made it easy to regard [Thomas Aquinas] humorously as a sort of walking wine-barrel, common in the comedies of so many nations; he joked about it himself. It may be that he, and not some irritated partisan of the Augustinian or Arabian parties, was responsible for the sublime exaggeration that a crescent was cut out of the dinner table to allow him to sit down."[22]

In any case, Aquinas repeatedly invokes this inordinate desire as he tries, like Augustine, to take necessity, real hunger, and health out of the formula that distinguishes between the human animal who needs to eat in order to live and the gluttonous sinner who lives to eat. An inordinate desire, he explains, is one that makes us depart from the path of reason, which is the regulator and guarantee of moral virtue. In any case, the novice overeater can relax, because if one overindulges through inexperience—because of a hazy or otherwise inaccurate idea of how much food is necessary—that is not gluttony. "It is a case of gluttony only when a man knowingly exceeds the measure in eating, from a desire for the pleasures of the palate."[23] And Aquinas returns to the notion that the sinfulness of gluttony lies in its ability to distract man from his final end—and from the love of, and the pure dedication to, God.

Warnings such as Aquinas's against excess and obsession were also invoked by church fathers not only in regard to the rogue monk tempted to eat more than his share but also in reference to the opposite case—that is, nuns (for they were almost always nuns) who succumbed to the equally disturbing and disruptive temptation to indulge in excessive fasting. These women, whom the historian Rudolph M. Bell has termed "holy anorexics," punished their bodies by starving themselves and indulging in all manner of inventive and frequently disgusting self-mortifications.[24] Though a number of them—Saint Catherine of Siena, Saint Clare of Assisi, Saint Veronica—were eventually canonized, in their lifetimes they troubled the ecclesiastical authorities, who cautioned them to be on guard against the sin of pride: the self-satisfaction they might derive from the pain and the heroic discomfort they managed to endure.

In sum, then, the specter of gluttony was never meant to prevent the faithful from eating. Although the pious were duly warned against the insidious ways in which concuspiscence and pleasure could masquerade as necessity, the early Christian theologians had a surprising and comparatively (that is, compared to their often extreme views on sex and the lures of lust) tolerant attitude toward the occasional overindulgence. The sin of gluttony *was* one of degree, but the degree that appeared to matter most was not so much excessive consumption as excessive appetite, desire, and attention: the fixation on food, the pleasure derived from taste; the self-inflicted pain of starvation; and, especially, the ways in which all these related fixations turned one's attention away from the more important and urgent needs of the soul and the spirit.

Too soon, too delicately, too expensively, too greedily, too much. If we use this yardstick—together with that of excessive preoccupation and *inordinate interest*—to identify the sin and the sinner, it becomes obvious that though gluttony appears to have become the least harmful of sins, it may well be the most widespread. Precisely because of our inordinate interests, our preoccupation with sampling the trendiest dishes at the costliest new restaurants, and our apparently paradoxical, obsessive horror of obesity, we have become a culture of gluttons.

CHAPTER TWO

The Wages of Sin

A little boy and his mother are on line at the supermarket behind an overweight woman.

> *"Mommy," says the little boy. "That lady is fat."*
> *"Shush," says his mother. "She'll hear you."*
> *"But mommy, she's so fat."*
> *"Be quiet, you don't want to hurt her feelings."*
> *After awhile the fat woman's beeper goes off.*
> *"Mommy, mommy," cries the little boy. "Watch out! She's backing up!"*

For many years, we've had on the wall above our dining room table a framed poster we bought in Tuscany more than a decade ago. The image is taken from the fresco cycle *The Last Judgment,* painted in the late fourteenth century by Taddeo di Bartolo on the walls of the cathedral of San Gimignano.

It's a nightmare vision of gluttons suffering in hell. Six sinners—in their former lives, big eaters—are gathered around a table covered with a white cloth. The damned, four men and two women, are naked, and all have bodies that testify to the sin responsible for the eternity they are now spending in the dining room in hell. The men have huge bellies, fleshy arms and backs; one has pendulous breasts. The women seem less obese than hefty and muscular; still, by fourteenth-century standards of female beauty, they are dauntingly Amazonian.

On the table are decanters of wine, glasses, round loaves of bread, and in the center a platter on which there is a plump, rather lonely looking, chicken. The damned stare, transfixed, at the food, their faces masks of desire, avidity, horror, and pain. Because standing in a sort of second tier, surrounding the circle of gluttons, is a small band of demons with a remarkable resemblance to Maurice Sendak's Wild Things. But this is not Sendak's "wild rumpus;" there's nothing playful about these devils. Their job is preventing the gluttons—by holding their arms and heads with their sharp talons and claws, by prodding them with bats and clubs—from getting anywhere near the food they crave. On one side of the anguished group, a horned monster grabs the arms of the man with the breasts and pins them behind his back.

On the ground, in front of the table, is the man who seems the most acutely aware of his sad fate and who appears to be taking it hardest. His body is twisted and malformed; neither his rib cage nor his genitals are where, anatomically, they should be. It's almost as if his body—flesh itself—has become a mockery of the desires that once drove him. A serpent coils around his upper torso and arms. Unable to stand the sight of the meal at which his companions are gazing with such longing, he bows his head in a posture of grief and covers his face with his hands.

On our poster, beneath the image—which, as it happens, rather closely resembles yet another depiction of sinners in hell, Fra Beato Angelico's later *The Last Judgment*—is a caption supplied by the regional tourist board of San Gimignano, *Mangiare bene a San Gimignano non e peccato.* To eat well in San Gimignano is not a sin.

But if it's not a sin in San Gimignano, where *is* it a sin? Nowhere, is the only logical answer one can possibly conclude. Surely (the poster slyly suggests) when the church talks about gluttony, it doesn't mean *Mangia bene*, eating well. Eating well, as every Italian knows, is a major reason to live, every human's birthright. Indeed, eating well is nothing less than a moral and social duty.

So why should we be surprised if Catholic Church officials (including, as we have seen, Thomas Aquinas) responded to the promptings of this sense of duty. For centuries, writers—among them, Chaucer and Rabelais—have made fun of clerics who preach against gluttony and then, the moment their sermons end, race out of the church before their sumptuous Sunday lunches have a chance to get cold. The alleged gluttonousness of priests was, for centuries, a sort of cultural given, part urban legend, part fact, part cliché, part projection—and the subject of enormous fascination and speculation.

In fact, there was a certain amount of truth in these allegations. During the Middle Ages, the clergy regularly indulged in a sort of ritualized gluttony, setting aside certain holidays—most notably the Feast of Fools, a chaotic overturning of the traditional order that took place on Innocents' Day, the 28th of December—for a blowout of food and drink that might go on for days.

Quite apart from the feasts ordained by liturgical and ritual calendars, Western European clerics were known for their capacity to eat. According to the Roman Curia, priests in the north of Italy—in spite of the order to eat "normal amounts"—actually ate Pantagruelesque portions. As late as 1059, reminders were issued at the Lateran Synod of the apparently unforgettable excesses that had taken place at a church conference in Aachen in 816.[25]

In our own era, in contemporary Rome, a popular piece of tourist advice counsels that if you happen to find yourself in the vicinity of the Vatican, around lunchtime, you should find a group of Jesuits and the Dominicans and go where they go, eat in the restaurants where they eat, order what they order. In these jokes about the eating and drinking habits of priests, cynicism about the piety of gourmands is admixed with sly admiration for men who have, in theory, abjured the temptations of the world and still know how to live pleasurably in that very same world. Surely, such men of God show us with their actions, with their very bodies, that eating well is *not* really a sin. And not just in San Gimignano.

Like Taddeo di Bartolo and Fra Angelico, Dante thought otherwise. For even as the theologians were codifying the offenses for which one could be sent to the less salutary and welcoming regions of the afterlife, visionary artists and writers were turning their imaginations loose on the subject of what sinners could expect to find there.

In the sixth canto of the *Inferno,* the gluttons are consigned to the third circle of hell, to a lower region and a more hideous fate than the lustful, whose sin resembles their own in its violation of the principles of continence and moderation. But—in the ranking contest that has determined the hierarchy of sin—the gluttons have outdone the lechers in the beastliness and the sheer animal grossness of their vices. At least the lustful have fixed their worshipful attentions on each other. What have the gluttons worshiped? Their roast chickens, their wine, their bellies.

In Dante's hell, the gluttons shiver in the eternal foul weather—cold, lashing rain, hail, and snow—that has turned the ground into a stinking bog. Watched over by Cerberus, the three-headed dog, the gluttons howl like dogs themselves, twisting and turning in search of comfort or shelter, striving to protect themselves and each other from the cruel climate to which they have been doomed for eternity. Endless physical discomfort is their punishment for having wasted their lives pursuing the pleasures of the flesh.

The hells that Dante and di Bartolo imagined for the glutton were, if such fine distinctions can be made, fractionally less unpleasant than another prevailing notion, which became popular in the Middle Ages and extended into the Renaissance. This was the idea that gluttons would be appropriately damned to an eternity of the most disgusting conceivable diet. According to the *Book of God's Providence*, a fifteenth-century manual of virtues and vices that is thought to have been read by, and to have influenced, Hieronymus Bosch, the round table around which the former gluttons gather is burning hot, warmed by the same hellfire that makes the sinners so thirsty and hungry that they beg for straw to eat, for urine to drink, for excrement to devour. But all this is merely the appetizer, the prelude to the hellish meal proper. Next on the menu come frogs, vermin, lizards. A whole array of hideous creatures constitute the dinner that demons poke and prod and torture the hesitant, newly squeamish former gluttons into consuming.

Of course, once-pious Christians knew what awaited them as a consequence of overeating, they realized how important it was to watch their diets, how carefully they had to control their appetites. As these dire warnings and forecasts from the world of the dead exerted their pessimistic influence on the world of the living, gluttony began to seem more serious and more deadly. The promise of a good meal would surely have paled, at least slightly, when those about to eat it considered the punishment options they might expect: terrible aching hunger within sight of the unreachable red wine and golden roast chicken, stuffing one's belly with rats and slimy worms, or lying naked in the wet, cold rain with no way to get inside, and the knowledge that this suffering would last forever and ever and ever. What a risk we are taking as we reach for that glazed doughnut! No wonder that thoughtful and even altruistic humans have found it increasingly important to warn their peers about the passing, transient, gluttonous pleasure that leads to eternal penance and pain.

Perhaps the hardest thing for us to understand as more or less secular citizens of the twenty-first century is that, for the people of the Middle Ages, hell was not a metaphor but a reality the pious could picture all too clearly. Those who had trouble visualizing or who suffered from limited imaginations were reminded by the decorations that adorned the doorways and chapels of their cathedrals. One such bas relief, on the main portal of the cathedral of Orvieto, depicts the punishments of the damned in hell—a theme that is repeated in the paintings in the church's interior.

Scholars have demonstrated that in the Middle Ages cyclical famines and periods of relative privation were followed by intervals during which people ate as if there were no tomorrow. Thus, much of the population behaved like gluttons for a short, happy season of the year. At the start of their feasts, the still sober, still hungry revelers would have had a brief glimpse of the road down which they were heading. Or perhaps that was part of the point of the feast, and certainly of the drunkenness involved: to briefly escape the knowledge of the hardness of life in this world and the cruelty of the life to come. Perhaps fear and guilt might even have worked as a spice, seasoning the glutton's meal with abandon and terror.

Your mama is so fat she had to be baptized in Sea World.

Your mama is so fat that when she goes out to eat, she looks at the menu and says, "okay."

Along with lust, gluttony is perhaps the most easily depicted, the most visual of the deadly sins. How much simpler it is for the painter to show the glutton at his overloaded table, surrounded by an overabundance of food, than it is to show the more interior, more purely psychological failings of the envious or the proud.

By the late Middle Ages, gluttony had become a theme on which the artist was encouraged to let his imagination run wild. As always, the fantasies of Hieronymus Bosch ran considerably wilder than those of his contemporaries or his successors.

In Bosch's painting *The Last Judgment,* the gluttons have become food, doomed by one of hell's heavy-handed ironies: the eaters are being eaten. In the background, a stew of sinners—with the upturned faces of baby birds and the rapt looks of the newly baptized—is burbling in a giant cauldron over a roaring fire. So much for the soup course! In the foreground are two demons who could pass for elderly grandmas, except the one in the black babushka has a bird's legs for arms and a giant swollen belly, and the other old dame in a wimple has a lizard's feet. The creature in the wimple holds a large sauté pan in which we can discern a man's head, his hand, and one leg up to his knee. He is gazing directly at us, and he doesn't look happy. Beside the pan are two eggs. Are we going to have an omelet? How nicely it will go with the filet of the naked man, who is lying there, trussed, his hands crossed modestly over his genitals; his demeanor is strangely placid considering he's attached to a spit with a horrifyingly convincing and lovingly rendered rotisserie feature. You can see the mechanism, exactly how it would turn. Meanwhile Babushka douses the man from a little saucier, presumably to tenderize and flavor the final product.

Brueghel's vision of gluttony is nearly as energetic but notably less sadistic than Bosch's. Except for Brueghel's rendering of *Lust,* which delivers a succession of small shocks each time you look closely enough to see what people are actually doing with their hands, their genitals, and their bodies, *Gluttony* (*Gula,* or *Throat*) is the most animate of the series of drawings (to be later used for engravings) in which he depicted the seven deadly sins. The caption across the bottom of Brueghel's design warns, "Shun drunkenness and gluttony, because excess makes man forget God and himself." Surely, the monsters of gluttony in this demonic landscape have their minds (or what's left of their minds) on all manner of things instead of their Heavenly Father.

At yet another round table are two naked women. One is draining a jug of wine while the second sprawls wantonly and shamelessly across the lap of a nearly faceless man. In the foreground, Gula herself—the personification of the gaping

1. Saint Gregory dictating to a Scribe, Manuscript, Cod. Plut. III, sin. 9c, fol. 1r.
Biblioteca Laurenziana, Florence, Italy © Alinari, Regione Umbria, Art Resource, NY

2. Joos van Ghent (c.1435–c.1480). Thomas Aquinas (1225–1274).
Louvre, Paris, France © Erich Lessing / Art Resource, NY

3. Sodoma (1477–1549). Scenes from the life of Saint Catherine of Siena:
the swooning of the saint.
San Domenico, Siena, Italy © Scala / Art Resource, NY

4. Paul Delaroche (1797–1856). Saint Veronica.
Louvre, Paris, France © Réunion des Musées Nationaux / Art Resource, NY

5. Sandro Botticelli (1444–1510). Saint Augustine, 1480.
Fresco. Chiesa di Ognissanti, Florence, Italy © Scala / Art Resource, NY

6. Diego Rivera (1866–1957). Capitalist Dinner (La cena capitalista).
Secretaría de Educación Pública, Mexico City, D.F., Mexico
© Schalkwijk / Art Resource, NY

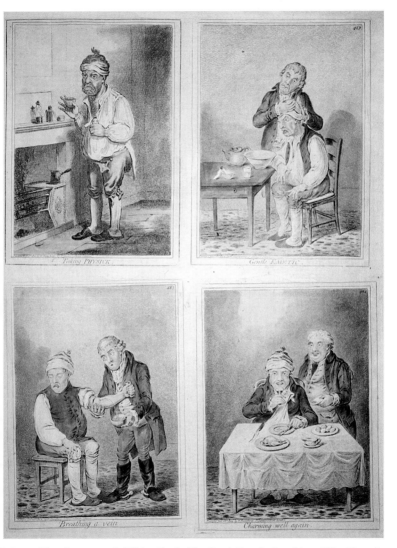

7. James Gilray (1757–1815). Taking Physic: The Gentle Emetic; Breathing a Vein; Charming well again, 1804. Private Collection © Image Select / Art Resource, NY

8. Mihaly Zichy (1827–1906). Before the orgy.
© Fine Art Photographic Library, London / Art Resource, NY

throat—sucks on a wine bottle like an infant at its mother's breast. One man vomits over the side of a bridge into the river below, while a demon holds his head as one would hold the head of a sick child, a tender enough picture except for the creature's beaked, hooded visage, and for the fact that the cascade of vomit is narrowly missing another man, who is swimming in the water. Men and beasts appear to belong to the same gluttonous species. Rising on two legs, a disturbingly reptilian dog grabs a cup between its jaws just as the cup tips off the edge of a plank that a porter is carrying on his back. One man has fallen backward into a keg of wine, almost everyone and everything is greedily gulping and slurping. The entire scene communicates the desperate, chaotic, overt, or barely suppressed violence of an R. Crumb cartoon, charged by a version of Crumb's unease about the frayed, thin reins of control that the mind exerts over the body.

Is this hell? Not exactly. It too closely resembles the world we know, and the disposition of power between humans and demons is not so well defined as it is in Bartolo or Bosch. In effect, the punishment is meted out by the gluttons themselves; it's not the eternity of hellfire they suffer but rather the awfulness of allowing their animal natures to triumph. What is depicted is not how the gluttons will suffer in the afterlife, but rather how unappealing they look in the here and now.

Something very similar—the sheer unesthetic unattractiveness and the social uselessness of gluttony—is what Spenser emphasizes when the seven deadly sins stage their grim and fantastic parade through the pages of *The Faerie Queene*. The passage depicting gluttony is so marvelously extreme, so exhilarating in its horror, in its desire, and in its ability to conjure up disgust that it deserves to be quoted in full:

> And by his side rode loathsome Gluttony,
> Deformed creature, on a filthie swyne;
> His belly was up-blowne with luxury,
> And eke with fatnesse swollen were his eyne,
> And like a Crane his necke was long and fyne,
> With which he swallowed up excessive feast,
> For want whereof poore people oft did pyne;
> And all the way, most like a brutish beast,
> He spued up his gorge, that all did him deteast.
>
> In green vine leaves he was right fitly clad;
> For other clothes he could not weare for heat,
> And on his head an yvie girland had,
> From under which fast trickled downe the sweat:
> Still as he rode, he somewhat still did eat,
> And in his hand did beare a bouzing can,

Oft which he supt so oft, that on his seat

His dronken corse he scarse upholden cans,

In shape and life more like a monster, than a man.

Unfit he was for any worldly thing,

And eke unhable once to stirre or go;

Not meet to be of counsell to a king,

Whose mind in meat and drinke was drowned so,

That from his friend he seldome knew his fo:

Full of diseases was his carcas blew,

And a dry dropsie through his flesh did flow:

Which by misdiet daily greater grew:

Such one was *Gluttony,* the second of that crew.[26]

This emphasis on the sheer distastefulness and nastiness of Gluttony—rather than on its consequences for the life beyond—is for the most part what characterizes modern depictions of the vice. By the time James Ensor drew his version of the sin of gluttony, the transgression had not only moved from the realm of the dead into the world of the living but also out of the landscape and into the private domain—in fact, to the dinner table, where gluttony so often makes its unwelcome appearance. In Ensor's rendition, two gross, ugly men—one fat, the other skinny and with a long twisted nose that suggests a red cruller—sit at a table in front of a platter on which there is a scrawny bird that seems to be, dismayingly, still alive and still possessed of most of its feathers.

The thin man slumps back in his chair, his fat friend grasps his eating utensils and leans on the table. Behind them on the wall is a painting—a painting within a painting—of a farm scene in which barnyard animals are being slaughtered. A sheep is being eviscerated, the innards and intestines yanked from its body, while a somewhat disconsolate dog stands nearby, and a pig lies on the ground, either about to suffer or just having suffered the same fate as the sheep. But what's most appalling is not the sheep guts, or the sodden, awful faces of the gluttonous revelers, but rather the fact that two diners sharing their riotous meal appear to be eating and vomiting at the same time. What's worst of all is the accuracy with which Ensor has captured a state of being. He has discovered the visual equivalent for precisely how it feels when you've eaten so much that you think you're about to be sick and still can't stop eating.

More recently the caveat that has superseded the threats of eternal hell is the threat of death itself. The idea that overeating presents a health risk is, of course, nothing new. It occurred to Renaissance writers who concerned themselves with the subjects of food and health,

> For the individual who succumbs to surfeit and riotous excess,
> "worshipping the belly as God," disaster awaits. For one, the

internal heat is suffocated and food begins to decay, accidentally generating its own putrescent heat. Sooty fumes build up, and the viscera swells. The fumes then fill the head, dulling our eyesight and thoughts. Then they diffuse throughout the body, causing intense weariness, and the flesh absorbs this corrupt matter. Paradoxically, the body then wastes away, having received no assimilatable nutrients. . . . With time, the corrupt matter collects in the muscles and kidneys, causing the all too familiar gout and kidney stones, of all, the sense of taste is eventually totally obscured, and gluttons search in vain for ever more delectable morsels, overstimulating their appetites, and finally eating themselves to death.[27]

For centuries, it was thought that a single eating binge could prove fatal—the Princess of Palatine (a member of the court of Louis XIV) and Henry Thrale, a close friend of the eighteenth-century writer Samuel Johnson—were among the more well known figures believed to have suffered death by overindulgence.

Now, of course, we understand that this particular road to ruin is a slower and more circuitous one, that the distance is hard to travel in a single night of dedicated eating. Yet, though we no longer fear the catastrophic effects of a single meal, the concern—and the paranoia—about the health consequences of what and how much we eat has never been so intense. We're barraged with reminders that overeating is unhealthy, that a poor diet is one of the major contributing factors to a prodigious and daunting range of ordinary, exotic, and fatal diseases. We know what our grandparents didn't know—about the horrors of cholesterol, the perils of red meat, the liver-destroying effects of wine, the artery-clogging power of the foods (bacon, butter, ice cream) that are most delicious.

Our obsession with living forever means that we are doubly affronted by the spectacle of the obese, whose flesh seems to be making a statement that the pleasures of the moment have been chosen over the promise of longevity. Doesn't that fat man want to *live?* The so-called glutton is a walking rebuke to our self-control, our self-denial, and to our shaky faith that if we watch ourselves, if we do this and don't do that, then surely death cannot touch us.

> *Did you hear the one about the fat guy who asked directions to the number six train and the conductor told him he'd probably be better off taking the number three train twice?*
> *Did you hear the one about the fat lady who wore a yellow raincoat and people kept waving their arms at her because they thought she was a taxi?*

Published in 1982, *Psychological Aspects of Obesity: A Handbook,* edited by Benjamin Wolman, Ph.D., with Stephen deBerry, Ph.D., offers an informative overview of the way in which the wages of gluttony are perceived by the helping professions. As the book makes clear, psychotherapists—and the wider scientific community—are much less likely than the general public to ascribe every case of obesity to the sorts of behaviors and indulgences traditionally associated with gluttony—greediness, laziness, and forth. The articles collected here also take into account genetic factors, socioeconomic and cultural influences, as well as the possibility that the brains of obese humans may have some biological resemblance to those of laboratory animals with hypothalmic brain lesions. In fact, in the decades since this volume was published, more and other scientific studies have concentrated on the biological and psychological nature of obesity, so that it's rare these days to pick up the science section of the newspaper or to tune in the evening news without reading or hearing about some new research into the organic, cellular, or hereditary causes and triggers of overweight.

But, as its title promises, the book's main focus is obesity's *psychological* aspects. In a series of chapters culled from essays and papers by experts in the field, the handbook considers such topics as the relation between depression and obesity, the etiology of obesity in adolescence, the problems faced by the obese in maintaining a "normal" weight, and the tendencies and attitudes—a misdirected drive for power, feelings of guilt and inferiority, distorted body image, and forth—that might predispose someone to become obese in the first place. The second half of the collection addresses itself to the efficacy of various modes of therapy: psychoanalysis, behavioral therapy, group therapy, and hypnosis.

Included are case histories in which the psyche of an obese person is probed to reveal the root causes of a problematic and uncontrollable weight gain. One man who endured a terrible childhood and who is trapped in a no less awful married life eats, it is suggested, to make himself so unhappy that his unsympathetic wife will begin to feel sorry for him and fall in love with him and be inspired to prove that she cares. In another case, an overweight woman is eating to compensate for—surprise—the inadequacies and emotional frigidity of her chilly, rejecting parents.

What goes without saying is how far we've come from the image of the devil tempting the sinner with pies and cakes, plying the glutton with the joys of the table as a substitute for—a dangerous distraction from—the more profound rewards of the spirit. For all the intensity of the medieval debate about the nature of predestination and free will, no one seems to have doubted that the glutton had a choice concerning when, what, and how much to eat—how far and how vehemently to resist the devil. At the same time, early philosophers had remarkably little interest in *why* the glutton overate—or perhaps it was merely assumed that the glutton *liked* eating.

But now that we are more likely to believe in some form of free will, we are paradoxically more willing to believe that eating or not eating is a response to something that happens outside of ourselves, something that was done to us, and that we must struggle to overcome. It's revealing of our psychotherapeutic view of humanity and of our blame-based culture that we are so persuaded that the quality and quantity of what we ingest is primarily reactive, that our eating habits are less a matter of will and agency than one of displaced response to an injury or harm we have suffered, more often than not in the distant past.

Each year, dozens of books are published to help victims of eating disorders solve the perilous riddle of their problems with food. One of the earliest was Kim Chernin's *The Obsession,* which first appeared in 1981, a pioneer exploration of the self-loathing and the paralyzing guilt and shame and terror that women in our culture so often feel for their own less than "perfect" bodies. Chernin finds a host of partial explanations for certain women's inability to get through a single day without consulting the bathroom scale. She suggests a range of causes for this widespread fixation, ranging from primal loathing of the female body that may be endemic in the species to destructive parental and familial influences, from the widespread societal and cultural emphasis on thinness to the expectations of individual men who respond with horror when their wives or girlfriends gain weight. She tracks her own familiarity with compulsive eating to a day when she was 17, living in Berlin: "I am not hungry. I had pushed away my plate moments before. But my hand is reaching and I know that I am reaching for something that has been lost. . . . Suddenly it seems to me that nothing will ever still this hunger—an immense implacable craving that I do not remember having felt before.

"Suddenly, I realize that I am putting too much butter on my breakfast roll. I am convinced that everyone is looking at me. I put down the butter knife. I break off a piece of roll and put it in my mouth. But it seems to me that I am wolfing it down." After running out of the house, still gnawing on her roll, she cut the line waiting to buy sausage at a shop, darts in front of the man in front of her, and runs down the street, eating her sausage.

"And so I ran from bakery to bakery, from street stall to street stall, buying cones of roasted chestnuts, which made me frantic because I had to peel away the skins. I bought a pound of chocolate and ate it as I ran. I never went to the same place." She gets a mesh bag in which to carry her food, and finds herself eating on park benches, trying to chew at a normal rate, as if she is having a picnic instead of satisfying a compulsion. Only much later, after succumbing to successive cycles of binging and dieting, does Chernin have a revelation:

"What I wanted from food was companionship, comfort, reassurance, a sense of warmth and well-being that was hard for me to find in my own life, even in my own home. And now that these emotions were coming to the surface, they could no longer easily be satisfied with food. I was hungering, it was true; but food apparently was not what I was hungering for."[28]

Among the writers who have followed in Chernin's path—and benefited from similar epiphanies—is Geneen Roth, whose books are enormously popular and who frequently leads well-attended workshops for people who suffer from eating disorders. In her third book, *When Food Is Love,* Roth reports on how falling in love made her confront the ways in which food functioned for her as a substitute for intimacy; she describes how, after overcoming her negative attitudes toward food, she was finally able to experience true love:

> Diets don't work because food and weight are the symptoms, not the problems. The focus on weight provides a convenient and culturally reinforced distraction from the reasons why so many people use food when they are not hungry. These reasons are more complex than—and will never be solved with—will power, counting calories, and exercise. They have to do with neglect, lack of trust, lack of love, sexual abuse, physical abuse, unexpressed rage, grief, being the object of discrimination, protection from getting hurt again. People abuse themselves with food because they don't know they deserve better. People

abuse themselves because they've been abused. . . . Because our patterns of eating were *formed* by early patterns of loving, it is necessary to understand and work with both food and love to feel satisfied with our relationship to either.[29]

Perhaps what's most striking about both of these passages, and about the books from which they're taken, is how little discussion, how little acknowledgment there is of the possibility that one might find genuine pleasure in eating, and even overeating. How different Kim Chernin's account of her consumption of chocolate is from the prose that might result if a writer like, say, M. F. K. Fisher were to address the subject of a sausage and chocolate meal.

During the Middle Ages and the Renaissance, it was a cultural given that the taste for fine food and excessive drink was a glutton's downfall. But by the end of the twentieth century, food had come to mean compensation, comfort, the hoped-for release from suffering, the whole list of interpretations that Geneen Roth suggests. To some degree, this widespread uneasiness about nourishment and consumption reflects the shifts in world demographics, and the ways in which patterns of shortage and surfeit, wealth and poverty manifest themselves and affect the citizens of rich and poor nations. One can hardly imagine a starving citizen of a third-world country facing the sorts of struggles that challenge Americans like Kim Chernin and Geneen Roth. Indeed, visitors from developing countries are often confused by the fact that in the United States the rich are more likely to be thin while the poor often tend toward overweight.

For many Americans, especially women tormented by the skeletal standards of beauty that the media purveys, food has become the enemy—but a very different sort of foe than it must have been to the medieval glutton. And nowhere, or rarely, in these books, do we find the sensuous appreciation of food, the joyous rapt attention with which a writer such as, say, Henry Miller, describes a memorable meal.

In addition to the guilt, the sense of a loss of control, and of course the reasonable health risks and concerns connected with eating disorders of all sorts, those who exceed the unforgiving norms our culture has established for the human body are subjected to semiconstant small and large doses of insult and humiliation, of casual and institutionalized prejudice and discrimination. Perhaps the most interesting chapter in *Psychological Aspects of Obesity* is an essay, written by Natalie Allon, entitled "The Stigma of Overweight in Everyday Life," which examines the ways in which the obese are made to see themselves not merely as inferior and marginalized but as deviant and wicked.

Presumably, anyone who has ever attended grade school or spent time with small children or merely watched children interact with other children will have observed the mercilessness with which the young treat their chubby classmates. Given that adolescence is not the stage at which we are at our kindest and most tolerant, we can safely assume that the life of most obese teenagers is an unenviable one. Yet thanks to the behavioral scientists' zeal for researching, documenting, and precisely quantifying what some might consider self-evident, studies proved that "children responded in very unfavorable ways to silhouettes of endomorphic children," and that "86 percent of those children who were consistent in their choices showed an aversion for chubbiness when tested with headless photographs of chubby, average, and thin children in bathing suits."[30]

What's more revealing—and even more upsetting—is the evidence concerning the obstacles and insults the obese adult is obliged to face on a more or less daily basis. The damage inflicted by the cruelty and contempt with which the overweight are routinely burlesqued in the media pales in comparison to the harm caused by the discrimination they face in the process of gaining admission to college and finding a job. Employers, it has been shown, not only tend to assume that a fat person will be less reliable, energetic, and efficient, but are reluctant to hire the overweight for positions (receptionists, etc.) in which their size might affront the delicate sensibilities of potential customers and the general public. Fat people often have difficulty in getting health insurance and in obtaining adequate medical care, for many doctors (as yet more studies have demonstrated) display an unseemly and unprofessional dismissiveness towards their over-weight patients.

In addition, the obese often find it challenging to carry out the sort of quotidian activities that most of us take for granted: buying clothes, sitting comfortably in theaters, on airplanes, trains, and buses, and even getting through turnstiles designed for the ectomorphic subway rider. Recently, Southwest Airlines passed a ruling requiring passengers over a certain weight to purchase two seats. In what is perhaps the most disturbing recent development of all, states have now begun to get tough on parents thought to be too lax about their children's diet. A three-year-old girl named Anamarie Martinez-Regino was taken from her home because her parents were unwilling or unable to persuade or force her to lose weight.

More and more often, we read articles and hear TV com-mentators advocating government intervention to protect us from the greed of a corporate culture that profits from our unhealthy attraction to sugary and fatty foods. Legal experts discuss the feasibility of mounting class action suits—on the model of the recent and ongoing litigation against so-called big tobacco companies—against fast-food restaurants, junk-food manufacturers, and advertisers who target children with ads for salty fried snacks and brightly colored candy masquerading as breakfast cereal.

What's slightly more disturbing is the notion that not only do fat people need to be monitored, controlled, and saved from their gluttonous impulses, but that we need to be saved from them— that certain forms of social control might be required to help the overweight resist temptation. Writing in the *San Francisco Chronicle,* essayist Ruth Rosen has suggested that such actions might be motivated by compassion for such innocent victims as the parents of a child whose overweight helped lead to diabetes, or the child of a parent who died from weight-related causes. Of course the bottom line is concern for our pocketbooks, for the cost—shared by the wider population—of treating those who suffer from obesity-related ailments. As a partial remedy, Rosen proposes that schools and employers might forbid the sale of junk food on campus and in offices. Finally, she suggests that, in a more glorious future, the host who serves his guests greasy potato chips and doughnuts will incur the same horrified disapproval as the smoker who lights up—and blows smoke in our faces.

Rosen is not alone in her belief that legislation may be required to regulate the social costs of overeating. A recent item on CBS worriedly considered the alarming growth in the number of overweight and obese young people—a group that now comprises 14 percent of American children. According to the news clip, overweight was soon expected to surpass cigarette smoking as the major preventable cause of death: each year, 350,000 people die of obesity-related causes. Thirteen billion dollars is spent annually on food ads directed at children, and four out of five ads are for some excessively sugary or fatty product. The problem is undeniable, but once more the projected solution gives one pause; several interviewees raised the possibility of suing the purveyors of potato chips and candy bars. How far we have come from Saint Augustine and John Cassian and Chrysostom, taking it for granted that the struggle against temptation would be waged in the glutton's heart and mind—and not, presumably, in the law courts.

You're so fat when they pierced your ears, they had to use a harpoon.
You're so fat you've got to put on lipstick with a paint roller.

In studies that have examined the causes and motives behind the stigmatization of the overweight, such prejudice has been found to derive from the widely accepted notion that fat people are at fault, responsible for their weight and appearance, that they are self-indulgent, sloppy, lazy, morally lax, lacking in the qualities of self-denial and impulse control that our society (still so heavily influenced by the legacy of Puritanism) values and rewards. In a 1978 book, *The Seven Deadly Sins: Society and Evil,* sociologist Stanford M. Lyman takes a sociocultural approach to the reasons why we are so harsh in our condemnation of the so-called glutton.

> The apparently voluntary character of food gluttony serves to point up why it is more likely to seem "criminal" than sick, an act of moral defalcation rather than medical pathology. Although gluttony is not proscribed by the criminal law, it partakes of some of the social sanctions and moral understandings that govern orientations toward those who commit crimes. . . . Gluttony is an excessive *self*-indulgence. Even in its disrespect for the body it overvalues the ego that it slavishly satisfies.[31]

Most of us would no doubt claim that we are too sensible, compassionate, and enlightened to feel prejudice against the obese. We would never tell the sorts of cruel jokes scattered throughout this chapter. But let's consider how we feel when we've taken our already cramped seat in coach class on the airplane and suddenly our seatmate appears—a man or woman whose excessive weight promises to make our journey even more uncomfortable than we'd anticipated. Perhaps, contemplating a trip of this sort, we might find ourselves inclined to support

Southwest Airline's discriminatory two-seats-per-large-passenger rule. Meanwhile, as we try not to stare at our sizable traveling companion, we might as well be the medieval monks glaring at the friar who's helped himself to an extra portion. For what's involved in both cases is our notion of one's proper share, of surfeit and shortage—not enough food in one case, not enough space in the other.

"The glutton is also noticeable as a defiler of his own body space. His appetite threatens to engulf the spaces of others as he spreads out to take more than one person's ordinary allotment of territory. If he grows too large, he may no longer fit into ordinary chairs . . . and require special arrangements in advance of his coming."[32] The glutton's "crime" is crossing boundaries that we jealously guard and that are defined by our most primitive instincts: hunger, territoriality—that is to say, survival.

So we come full circle back to the language of crime and innocence, sin and penance, guilt and punishment—a view of overweight frequently adopted and internalized by the obese themselves. "Many groups of dieters whom I studied," writes Natalie Allon, "believed that fatness was the outcome of immoral self-indulgence. Group dieters used much religious language in considering themselves bad or good dieters—words such as sinner, saint, devil, angel, guilt, transgression, confession, absolution, diet Bible—as they partook of the rituals of group dieting."[33] Nor does the association between gluttony and the language of religion exist solely in the minds of dieters, the obese, and the food-obsessed. In fact it's extremely common to speak of having overeaten as having "been bad"; rich, fattening foods are advertised as being "sinfully delicious"; and probably most of us have thought or confessed the fact that we've felt "guilty" for having eaten more than we should have.

Like the members of other Twelve-Step programs, and not unlike the medieval gluttons who must have felt inspired to repent and pray for divine assistance in resisting temptation, the members of Overeaters Anonymous employ the terminology of religion. *Lifeline,* the magazine of Overeaters Anonymous, is filled with stories of healing and recovery, first-person accounts in which God was asked to intercede, to provide a spiritual awakening, and to remove the dangerous and destructive flaws from the recovering overeater's character.

Routinely, the capacity to achieve sobriety and abstinence— which for OA members means the ability to restrict one's self to three healthy and sensible meals a day—is credited to divine mercy and love, and to the good effects of an intimate and sustaining relationship with God. In one testimonial, a woman reports that coming to her first meeting and identifying herself as a recovering compulsive eater was more difficult for her than to say that she was a shoplifter, a serial killer, or a prostitute. Only after admitting that she was powerless over food and asking for the help of a higher power was she at last able to end her unhappy career as a "grazer and a binger."

For perhaps obvious reasons, the term "gluttony" is now rarely used as a synonym for compulsive eating. Yet Stanford Lyman conflates the two to make the point that our culture's attitude toward the obese is not unlike an older society's view of the gluttonous sinner:

> Societal opposition to gluttony manifests itself in a variety of social control devices and institutional arrangements. Although rarely organized as a group, very fat individuals at times seem to form a much beset minority, objects of calculating discrimination and bitter prejudice. Stigmatized because their addiction to food is so visible in its consequences, the obese find themselves ridiculed, rejected, and repulsed by many of those who do not overindulge. Children revile them on the streets, persons of average size refuse to date, dance, or dine with them, and many businesses, government, and professional associations refuse to employ them. So great is the pressure to conform to the dictates of the slimness culture in America that occasionally an overweight person speaks out, pointing to the similarities of his condition to that of racial and national minorities.[34]

Indeed, the overweight have found a forum in which to speak out, at the meetings, conventions, and in the bimonthly newsletter sponsored by NAAFA—the National Association to Advance Fat Acceptance. A recent issue of the newsletter, available on the internet, calls for readers to write to the government to protest the National Institute of Health's ongoing studies of normal-sized children to find out if obesity might have a metabolic basis. There are directions for giving money and establishing a living trust to benefit NAAFA, reviews of relevant new books, a report on the Trunk Sale at a NAAFA gathering in San Francisco, an update on the struggle to force auto manufacturers to provide seat belts that can save the lives of passengers who weigh over 215 pounds, and an article on the problems—the fear of appearing in public in a bathing suit, the narrow ladders that often provide the only access to swimming pools—that make it more difficult for the overweight to get the exercise that they need. There is a brief discussion of how obesity should be defined, and another about the effectiveness of behavioral psychotherapy in helping patients lose weight. Finally, there are grateful letters from readers whose lives have been improved by the support and sustenance they gain from belonging to NAAFA.

Equally fervent—if somewhat less affirmative and forgiv-ing—are the gospel tracts, also available on-line. One of the most heartfelt and persuasive is the work of a preacher identified only as George Clark:

After conducting healing campaigns and mailing out thousands of anointed handkerchiefs—since 1930—I have learned that the greatest physical cause of sickness among the people of God is coming from this lust for overindulgence in eating. . . . Tens of thousands of truly converted people are sick and are suffering with heart trouble coming from high blood pressure and other ailments which result from overeating. . . . Did you ever wonder why artists have never depicted any of Jesus' disciples as being overweight or of the fleshy type? No one could have followed Jesus very long and remained overweight. . . . If eating too much has brought on high blood pressure, heart trouble, or many of the other diseases which come from being overweight, then God requires a reduction in your eating.

Given our perhaps misguided sense of living in a secular society, it's startling to find that our relationship with food is still so commonly translated directly into the language of God and the devil, of sin and repentance. But why should we be surprised, when we are constantly being reminded that our feelings about our diet and our body can be irrational, passionate, and closer to the province of faith and superstition than that of reason and science?

CHAPTER THREE

The Real Wages of Sin

According to the National Institute of Diabetes and Digestive and Kidney diseases, a branch of the National Institute of Health, one-third of all Americans—or approximately 63 million—are over-weight. Of these, 32 million are adult females, 26 million adult males, and 4.7 million are children and adolescents. According to a recent story on CBS, the percentage of American children who are obese is climbing at an alarming rate. Indeed, according to the CBS news item, broadcast on 20 June 2002, 14 percent of American children are overweight or obese. Every year, 350,000 deaths are attributable to poor diet and inactivity, and 70 percent of cardiovascular disease is related to excess weight. At any given time, 35 to 40 percent of American women and 20 to 24 percent of American men are dieting, and the amount they spend annually—quoted figures range from $33 to $55 billion—reflects the intensity and the cost of their efforts. The figure exceeds projections for the entire federal Education, Training, Employment, and Social Services budgets, and equals the gross national product of Ireland. According to a study of Optifast dieters, the cost per pound lost was $180.

Franchised in 27 countries, Weight Watchers International draws over a million people each week to its meetings. For the first 13 weeks of 2002, revenues rose 12 percent to $212.5 million dollars. Jenny Craig, another highly profitable weight loss company, reported revenues of $142.9 million in the last six months of 2001. For the upmarket consumer with reservations about the downscale appeal of such groups as Weight Watchers and Jenny Craig and wishing to lose weight quickly in a luxurious and more exclusive environment, the cost of a week's stay at The Golden Door, one of the oldest and most venerable health spas, near San Diego, California, is almost $6,000.

Given these statistics and considering the fortunes being made from our struggle against gluttony, we can safely assume the cultural emphasis on thinness is based on something more complex and insidious than esthetics or altruism. So it's hardly surprising that the media continues to bombard us with information about the dangers, the health risks, the psychological damage, and the social opprobrium faced by the unrepentant glutton.

On the other hand, it's probably impossible to tally the revenues earned as a consequence of our obsessive interest in food and our apparently unsatisfiable hunger: the annual incomes of fast food chains and fashionable five-star restaurants, the sales of such magazines as *Gourmet* and *Saveur*, cookbooks, kitchen equipment, and so forth.

Obviously, our culture exhibits a schizophrenic attitude toward gluttony. One minute, we're bombarded with images of food, advertisements for restaurants or the latest sweet or fatty snack, with recipes and cooking tips. A minute later, we're reminded that eating is tantamount to suicide, that indulgence and enjoyment equals social isolation and self-destruction. And someone is making money from both sides of our ambivalence about, and fascination with, food, diet, gluttony, and starvation.

In any case, it seems clear that of all the seven deadly sins, gluttony—with the exception, one assumes of greed—has become the most closely associated with large quantities of money, the most lucrative, the most profitable, the easiest to market.

More than any other living individual, Carnie Wilson—the daughter of former Beach Boy Brian Wilson and a member of the now disbanded singing group Wilson Phillips—embodies, so to speak, the ways in which our culture has come to view the glutton. No one, except perhaps for Oprah Winfrey, has had her struggles with overweight so closely followed by fans and detractors alike, and so widely publicized. What makes Wilson's case so unique is not only the degree to which her suffering has become spectacle, but the extent of her complicity in the hucksterism that has surrounded her travails.

The details of Carnie's story are available on a number of elaborate web sites that provide copious information about her painful and (or so we are led to believe) ultimately triumphant life history and, in the process, illustrate the ways in which this history is emblematic of the current view of gluttony. On one such site we learn that her childhood obesity was a response to her father's severe psychological problems. "For a little girl in desperate need of her father's attention, the distance became a chasm of confusion and pain. To ease her deep discomfort, Carnie turned to food."

Carnie was "always the heaviest person" in her class at school; at nine, she weighed 110 pounds. "Subject to the cool humiliation society visits on the obese," she was "teased unmercifully." The success of her singing group, Wilson Phillips, motivated Carnie to lose 90 pounds. But the pressures of a musical career caused her to resume overeating. "She wanted sugar. She wanted Hostess Cupcakes. She wanted Twinkies." Believing her weight gain had contributed to the eventual failure of Wilson Phillips, Carnie continued to binge, until she weighed 300 pounds.

By now, having so thoroughly violated the standards of the beauty culture, Carnie was embraced by the death culture and became an icon of disease, of the illnesses and disabilities that can befall the "morbidly obese" glutton. Her cholesterol level and her blood pressure rose; she experienced joint pain and shortness of breath. Realizing that she "was carrying a death sentence around on my back," she sought the help of Dr. Jonathan Sackier, who recognized at once that "she was invariably headed for heart disease, high blood pressure and coronary artery disease, diabetes, joint degeneration . . . skin problems and certain kinds of tumors. She was a walking time bomb with the clock ticking."

So, in August 1999, in San Diego, Carnie underwent laparoscopic gastric bypass surgery, an operation that was viewed live and in real time by 250,000 people. Since then, with the help and support of the weight-loss products marketed under the brand name of Changes, Carnie has remained thin—a success story that includes marriage in a wedding dress that had to be altered because she was still continuing to lose weight until the day of the ceremony. Her advice to those who wish to follow her example is: "Pay attention to what you *really* want. You have the power to change it" and to seek the help of The No Will Power Weight Loss Trio, a line of formulas including Thermo-Lift,

Changes NOW, and Power Nutrients Plus—all available for order on the internet.

Carnie Wilson's sad (or, in an alternate reading, triumphant) story illustrates the ways in which our culture has taken the difficulty of modifying our appetites and of coping with the demands of the body and transformed these private challenges into occasions for the public displays of self-recrimination and guilt, of sin, confession, and repentance—and into opportunities for earning and amassing prodigious sums of money.

Great Moments
in Gluttony

In her brilliant and beautifully written book, *An Alphabet for Gourmets*, M. F. K. Fisher explores the joys of overeating in a chapter entitled "G is for Gluttony":

> It is a curious fact that no man likes to call himself a glutton, and yet each of us has in him a trace of gluttony, potential or actual. I cannot believe that there exists a single coherent human being who will not confess, at least to himself, that once or twice he has stuffed himself to the bursting point, on anything from quail financiere to flapjacks, for no other reason than the

beastlike satisfaction of his belly. In fact I pity anyone who has not permitted himself this sensual experience, if only to determine what his private limitations are, and where, for himself alone, gourmandism ends and gluttony begins.[35]

Fisher goes on to offer a characteristically idiosyncratic defense of one of the great heroes of gluttony, Diamond Jim Brady, a railroad magnate of the Gilded Age, who—or so the story goes—would begin his meal by sitting six inches from the table and would quit only when his stomach rubbed uncomfortably against the edge. To that effect, he might consume, at a single dinner, dozens of oysters, some crabs, turtle soup, two ducks, several lobsters, a steak, rabbit, and just to keep healthy, various kinds of vegetables. For dessert he might eat an array of pastries and an entire box of chocolates.

Brady, claims Fisher, was not gluttonous, but rather gargantuan and "monstrous, in that his stomach was about six times normal size." He was, she notes, a member of a nearly extinct breed—big men, big eaters whose appetites mirrored their social and economic ambitions. She recalls with nostalgic affection her days as a schoolgirl, when she hoarded chocolate bars and ate seven or eight at once, together with a box of soda crackers, in a state of sheer "orgiastic pleasure."

Lately, she admits, her capacities for gluttony have diminished. Though she may accidentally overeat, she lacks the feverish appetite

9. 15th century CE. Gluttony and Abstinence; Le Livres des bonnes moeurs
by Jacques le Grant. Fol. 11. French, 15th c.
Musée Condé, Chantilly, France © Giraudon / Art Resource, NY

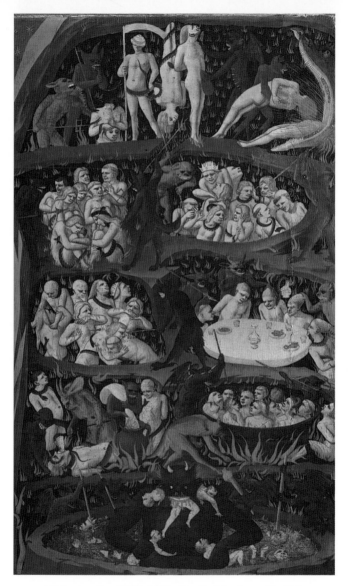

10. Fra Angelico (1387–1455). Detail of the damned in Hell,
from "The Last Judgment."
Museo di San Marco, Florence, Italy © Erich Lessing / Art Resource, NY

11. Giovanni da Modena (fl. 1409–1455). Hell. Detail. Fresco, ca. 1410.
San Petronio, Bologna, Italy © Scala / Art Resource, NY

12. Hieronymus Bosch (c. 1450–1516). Gluttony. Detail of "The Table of the Seven Deadly Sins."
Museo del Prado, Madrid, Spain © Erich Lessing / Art Resource, NY

13. Hieronymus Bosch (c. 1450–1516). Last Judgment. Central panel of triptych.
Akademie der Bildenden Künste, Vienna, Austria © Erich Lessing / Art Resource, NY

14. Pieter Brueghel the Elder (c. 1525–1569). Land of the Cockaigne (Land of Plenty).
Alte Pinakothek, Munich, Germany © Scala / Art Resource, NY

15. Jacob Jordaens (1593–1678). The Banquet of the Bean King, ca. 1655.
Musée d'Orsay, Paris, France © Erich Lessing / Art Resource, NY

16. Thomas Couture (1815–1879). The decadence of the Romans, 1847.
Musée d'Orsay, Paris, France © Erich Lessing / Art Resource, NY

of youth, a regrettable development she regards as symptomatic of her "dwindling powers." All that remains is an enduring weakness for a brief, gluttonous encounter with a great bottle of wine.

"As often as possible, when a really beautiful bottle is before me, I drink all I can of it, even when I know I have had more than I want physically. That is gluttonous. But I think to myself, when again will I have this taste upon my tongue. Where else in the world is there just such wine as this, with just this bouquet, at just this heat, in just this crystal cup. And when again will I be alive to it as I am this very minute, sitting here on a green hillside above the sea, or here in this dim, murmuring, richly odorous restaurant."[36] This always subversive and fresh writer alters our view of this deadly sin as a fast ticket to ill health or hell, and obliges us to acknowledge it as an affirmation of pleasure and of passion.

Though no one else has expressed it quite so plainly and eloquently, M. F. K. Fisher is certainly not alone in her view of gluttony—a perspective that goes somewhat beyond tolerance and acceptance to border on affection and admiration. This brings up perhaps the final contradiction in our attitude toward this deadly sin, an aspect it also shares in common (and alone) with lust. For unlike pride, envy, wrath—sins we can wholeheartedly condemn, sins that are hard to love—there's something about the serious glutton (or in any case, *some* serious gluttons) that inspires a certain respect for the life force—the appetite—

asserting itself in all that prodigious feasting. It's not unlike our secret feelings about various Don Juans and Casanovas; even as we understand the compulsive quality of their behavior and destructive effects it has on their hapless lovers, we can't help feeling a grudging regard for so much sheer sexual energy.

Traditionally, the subject of gluttony has served as an occasion to enumerate and celebrate the quantity and the deliciousness of the foods the glutton consumes. Many years ago, while waiting for a train, I sat beside two large, appealing women who were deeply engaged in a lively discussion of the difficulties of dieting—a conversation that was, I soon realized, a pretext to longingly and loving describe the pleasures of the fattening delights they felt compelled to avoid.

"I'm always doing fine," one of the women said, "until my niece comes over with a platter of that really crispy fried chicken. That salty skin is so hard to resist—"

"I can deal with that," said her friend. "It's my neighbor's devil's food cake. She uses a pound of butter in the icing alone." And so it went.

The women's conversation has countless literary antecedents. On the surface, as we have seen, the *Satyricon* is a satire about vulgarity, excess, and corruption. Beneath, like so many satires, it is a celebration—in this case of excess, food and wine, romantic intrigue, and sex. Most of it takes place at Trimalchio's feast, which—as it happens—was F. Scott Fitzgerald's working title for what would turn out to be *The Great Gatsby*. The connection, presumably, had to do with expensive party giving as a vehicle for, and a sign of, crossing social class borders. But the differences between the two books, particularly in their visions of enjoyment—big houses, drinking, social status, painful love affairs in Fitzgerald as opposed to gluttonous feasting and drinking, and theatrical homosexual romance in Petronius— make you glad Fitzgerald chose the title he did. Whatever lodges in your mind from your reading of *The Great Gatsby*, it has—it would be safe to say—little to do with eating.

But the food *is* what you remember about the party scene in *Satyricon*. Trimalchio's feast goes on and on and includes dancing, music, poetry; philosophical, literary, and metaphysical discussions; an extended reading from the records of Trimalchio's estate, a display of his household goods and gods—gods named Fat Profit, Good Luck, and Much Income. At one point, Trimalchio exhorts his guests to move their bowels if they wish to, presumably so they may be comfortable and ingest even more.

Ultimately, it's the menu that readers recall, and the approach to eating that defiantly raises every one of the red flags—*too soon, too delicately, too expensively, too greedily, too much*—that, for Gregory the Great, served as indicators of gluttony's wicked presence. Even before the "astrological course"—the array of delicacies (an African fig for Leo, two mullets for Pisces) chosen to represent each sign of the zodiac— the guests are treated to hors d'oeuvres served on a platter on which a wooden hen is sitting on a straw nest that is found to be full of pea hen's eggs. The guests are each handed spoons to crack open their eggs, which turn out to be made of rich pastry. The narrator—new to Trimalchio's sense of style—is about to throw his away when a warning from another guest inspires him to look more closely and he finds inside the egg a "fine fat oriole, nicely seasoned with pepper."

So it goes, in course after course, each more ingenious and over the top than the last. On another tray are "fat capons and sowbellies and a hare tricked out with wings to look like a little Pegasus, the corners of the tray stood four little gravy boats, all shaped like the satyr Marsyas, with phalluses for spouts and a spicy hot gravy dripping down over several large fish swimming about in the lagoon of the tray."[37]

In the Middle Ages and the Renaissance, even as artists like Bosch and Bartolo were depicting the gluttons' corner of hell, writers were transmuting popular legends into works such as the Cockaigne texts, verse and prose descriptions of the mythical Land of Cockaigne, a glutton's paradise where house walls are made of sausages, doors and windows of salmon, where the tabletops are pancakes, the roof rafters constructed of grilled eels.

The animals want nothing more from life than to be consumed in the most delicious dishes. The geese obligingly roast themselves, meat and fish prepare their own flesh for lunch, and rivers of wine and beer flow freely.

The paradisical landscape is reminiscent of the land of Bengodi, which Bocaccio refers to in one of the tales in *The Decameron*. There, the vines are tied with sausages, a goose and gosling can be bought for a farthing, a river of white wine flows beside a mountain of Parmesan cheese inhabited by people who do nothing all day but make macaroni and ravioli and live according to a guiding principle something like: the faster you eat the more you get.

Among the most famous celebrations of gluttony appear in the works of Rabelais, whose farcical descriptions of the daily regimens of Gargantua and his family are not unlike popular fantasies of the Land of Cockaigne. So, we learn, Gargantua's father

> Grandgousier was a fine tippler and a good friend, as fond of draining his glass as any man walking the earth, cheerfully tossing down salted tidbits to keep up his thirst. Which is why he usually kept a good supply of Mainz and Bayonne hams, plenty of smoked beef tongues, lots of whatever chitterlings were in season and beef pickled in mustard, reinforced by a special caviar from Provence, a good stock of sausages, not the ones

from Bologna (because he was afraid of the poisons Italians often use for seasoning), but those from Bigorre and Longaulnay (near Saint-Malo), from Brenne and Rouergue.[38]

Born after his mother Gargamelle ingests so much tripe that it sends her into labor, Gargantua carries on the family tradition. He

> sat down to table, and . . . began his meal with several dozen hams, smoked beef tongues, caviar, fried tripe, and assorted other appetizers. Meanwhile, four of his servants began to toss into his mouth, one after the other—but never stopping— shovelfuls of mustard, after which he drank an incredibly long draft of white wine, to make things easier for his kidneys. And then, eating whatever happened to be in season and he happened to like, he stopped only when his belly began to hang down. His drinking was totally unregulated, without any limits or decorum. As he said, the time to restrict your drinking was only when the cork soles of your slippers absorb enough so they swell half a foot thick.[39]

Though the effects of poverty are (or certainly were) among the most common literary subjects, and though many writers are (or at least were) familiar with the experience of running out of money and food, there are surprisingly few descriptions in literature of the effects of malnutrition and self-starvation. Of course, there's Knut Hamsun's novel, *Hunger*, and Kafka's story, "The Hunger Artist." But food, as it turns out, is far more likely to snag the writer's attention than is privation, and literature abounds in works that confirm the church father's worst fears about the degree to which overindulgence can fray and weaken the moral fiber.

The dinner scene that everyone remembers from Fielding's *Tom Jones* is in actuality a scene from the Tony Richardson film. In the book, Tom and Mrs. Waters do share a meal that functions as a prelude to a seduction. But it is not the seduction itself, as it is on film, and indeed Fielding makes the point that eating can function as a sort of anti-aphrodisiac, not only because it is so difficult to make love and eat at the same time, but because the pleasures of eating can distract one from romance. So the "insinuating air" of Mrs. Waters's sigh is "driven from (Tom's) ears by the coarse bubbling of some bottled ale, which at that time he was pouring forth . . . for as love frequently preserves us from the attacks of hunger, so hunger may possibly, in some cases, defend us against love." So it is not until dinner is over, until "the cloth was removed," that Mrs. Waters resumes her amorous and eventually successful assaults of Tom's shaky resolve to be faithful to his true love, Sophia.

With characteristic sly wit and grace, Fielding takes us through a sort of crash course in the history of gluttony—and a defense of hearty eating—on his way to explaining why Tom fails, at least temporarily, to respond to Mrs. Waters's advances:

> Heroes, notwithstanding any idea which, by means of flatterers, they may entertain of themselves, or the world may conceive of them, have certainly more of mortal than divine about them. However elevated their minds might be, their bodies at least (which is much the major part of most) are liable to the worst infirmities, and subject to the vilest offices of human nature. Among these latter, the act of eating, which hath by several wise men been considered as extremely mean and derogatory from the philosophic dignity, must be in some measure performed by the greatest prince, hero, or philosopher upon earth; nay, sometimes Nature hath been so frolicsome as to exact of these dignified characters a much more exorbitant share of this office than she hath obliged those of the lowest orders to perform.
>
> To say the truth, as no known inhabitant of this globe is really more than man, so none need be ashamed of submitting to what the necessities of man demand; but when those great personages I have just mentioned condescend to aim at confining such low offices to themselves—as when, by hoarding or destroying, they seem desirous to prevent others from eating— then they surely become very low and despicable.

Now, after this short preface, we think it no disparagement to our hero to mention the immoderate ardour with which he laid about him at this season. Indeed, it may be doubted whether Ulysses, who by the way seems to have had the best stomach of all the heroes in that eating poem of the Odyssey, ever made a better meal. Three pounds at least of that flesh which formerly had contributed to the composition of an ox was now honoured with becoming part of the individual Mr. Jones.

This particular we thought ourselves obliged to mention, as it may account for our hero's temporary neglect of his companion, who eat but very little, and was indeed employed in considerations of a very different nature, which passed unobserved by Jones, till he had entirely satisfied that appetite which a fast of twenty-four hours had procured him; but his dinner was no sooner ended than his attention to other matters revived; with these matters, therefore, we shall now proceed to acquaint the reader.[40]

Wry, sophisticated, exulting in its freedom to reexamine and redefine conventional morality, Fielding's defense of gluttony encapsulates much of what has been said on the subject, before and after Fielding's own lifetime, from Augustine and Aquinas through Chaucer and up to M. F. K. Fisher. At the same time, it seems as characteristic of the era in which it was written as the prose on the web site describing Carnie Wilson's ordeal seems typical of our own. Over the centuries, our notions of gluttony have evolved along with our ideas about food and the body, about society and the individual, about salvation and damnation, health and illness, life and death. However one praises or condemns this problematic and eternally seductive deadly sin, one thing seems clear: the broad, shiny face of the glutton has been—and continues to be—the mirror in which we see ourselves, our hopes and fears, our darkest dreams and deepest desires.

Notes

1. Saint Thaumaturgus Gregory, *Fathers of the Church: Life and Works*, trans. Michael Slusser, vol. 98. (Washington, D.C.: Catholic University of America Press, 1998).

2. Teresa M. Shaw, *The Burden of the Flesh: Fasting and Sexuality in Early Christianity* (Minneapolis: Fortress Press, 1998).

3. Ibid.

4. Saint Thomas Aquinas, *Summa Theologiae: A Concise Translation*, ed. Timothy McDermott (Allen Tex.: Christian Classics, 1991).

5. Geoffrey Chaucer, *The Works of Geoffrey Chaucer*, ed. F. N. Robinson (Boston: Houghton Mifflin, 1957), 150.

6. Ibid.

7. Ibid.

8. Ibid.

9. Ibid., 151.

10. William Langland, *The Vision of Piers Plowman* (Boston: Tuttle Publishing, 1995).

11. Herman Pleij, *Dreaming of Cockaigne*, trans. Diane Webb (New York: Columbia University Press, 2001), 372.

12. Aristotle, *The Nicomachean Ethics*, trans. David Ross (New York: Oxford University Press, 1998), 29.

13. Alexander Roberts and James Donaldson, eds., *The Ante-Nicene Christian Library: Translation of the Fathers Down to A.D. 325*, trans. Rev. S. Thelwall, vol. xviii. (Edinburgh: T&T Clark, 1866–72), 123–153.

14. Shaw, *Burden of the Flesh*, 133.

15. Saint Augustine, *The Confessions of Saint Augustine*, trans. Edward B. Pusey (New York: The Modern Library, 1949), 225.

16. Saint Augustine, *On Christian Doctrine*, trans. D. W. Robertson (New York: Liberal Arts Press, 1958).

17. Saint Augustine, *Confessions of Saint Augustine*, 226.

18. Saint Benedict, *The London Benedictine Rule* (Munich: Selbstverlag der Bayer, Benediktinerakademie, 1936).

19. Shaw, *Burden of the Flesh*, 75.

20. Saint Chrysostom and Phillip Schaff, *Saint Chrysostom: Homilies on the Gospel of St. John and the Epistle to the Hebrews (Nicene and Post-Nicene Fathers Series 1)* (Grand Rapids: William B. Eerdmans Publishing Co., 1984).

21. Ibid.

22. G. K. Chesterton, *Saint Thomas Aquinas* (New York: Image Books, 2001), 97.

23. Ibid.

24. Rudolph M. Bell, *Holy Anorexia* (Chicago: University of Chicago Press, 1985).

25. Pleij, *Dreaming of Cockaigne*, 133.

26. Edmund Spenser, *The Faerie Queene* (New York: E. P. Dutton & Company, 1964), 58.

27. Ken Albala, *Eating Right into the Renaissance* (Berkeley: University of California Press, 2002), 105.

28. Kim Chernin, *The Obsession* (New York: Harper Perennial, 1981), 4.

29. Geneen Roth, *When Food Is Love: Exploring the Relationship Between Eating and Intimacy* (New York: Plume, 1991), 4.

30. Benjamin Wolman, ed., *Psychological Aspects of Obesity: A Handbook* (New York: Van Nostrand Reinhold, 1982), 146.

31. Stanford M. Lyman, *The Seven Deadly Sins: Society and Evil* (New York: St. Martin's Press, 1978), 220.

32. Ibid., 223.

33. Wolman, *Aspects of Obesity,* 148.

34. Lyman, *Seven Deadly Sins,* 218.

35. M. F. K. Fisher, *The Art of Eating* (New York: Vintage, 1976), 613.

36. Ibid., 615.

37. Petronius, *The Satyricon,* trans. William Arrowsmith (New York: Meridian, 1994), 45.

38. François Rabelais, *Gargantua and Pantagruel,* trans. Burton Raffel (New York: W. W. Norton & Company, 1991), 14.

39. Ibid., 51.

40. Henry Fielding, *Tom Jones* (New York: The Modern Library, 1994), 419–20.

Bibliography

Albala, Ken. *Eating Right in the Renaissance*. Berkeley: University of California Press, 2002.

Augustine, Saint. *The Confessions of Saint Augustine*, trans. Edward B. Pusey, D. D. New York: The Modern Library, 1949.

Bell, Rudoph M. *Holy Anorexia*. Chicago: University of Chicago Press, 1985.

Chaucer, Geoffrey. *The Works of Geoffrey Chaucer*, ed. F. N. Robinson. Boston: Houghton Mifflin, 1957.

Chernin, Kim. *The Obsession*. New York: Harper Perennial, 1981.

Chesterton, G. K. *Saint Thomas Aquinas*. New York: Image Books, Doubleday, 2001.

Fielding, Henry. *Tom Jones*. New York: The Modern Library, 1994.

Fisher, M. F. K. *The Art of Eating*. New York: Vintage, 1976.

Lyman, Stanford M. *The Seven Deadly Sins: Society and Evil*. New York: St. Martin's Press, 1978.

Petronius. *The Satyricon*, trans. William Arrowsmith. New York: Meridian, 1994.

Pleij, Herman. *Dreaming of Cockaigne*, trans. Diane Webb. New York: Columbia University Press, 2001.

Rabelais, François. *Gargantua and Pantagruel*, trans. Burton Raffel. New York: W. W. Norton, 1991.

Roth, Geneen. *When Food Is Love.* New York: Plume, 1991.

Schwartz, Hillel. *Never Satisfied: A Cultural History of Fantasies and Fat.* New York: The Free Press, 1986.

Shaw, Teresa M. *The Burden of the Flesh: Fasting and Sexuality in Early Christianity.* Minneapolis: Fortress Press, 1998.

Spenser, Edmund. *The Faerie Queene.* New York: E. P. Dutton & Company, 1964.

Wolman, Benjamin, ed., with Stephen DeBerry, editorial associate. *Psychological Aspects of Obesity: A Handbook.* New York: Van Nostrand Reinhold, 1982.

Index